Once again Dr Derek Thomas serves up an appetising menu of good things in Praying the Saviour's Way. Here is a book that helps us to see that true prayer is about God and that the Lord's Prayer is a miniature seminar on living the Christian life. Instructive, practical, readable, challenging. Each chapter will make you eager for the next course. Nourishing fare indeed!

SINCLAIR B FERGUSON,
First Presbyterian Church, Columbia, South Carolina

'Do we only say our prayers, or do we really pray?' The adage may be old, but its challenge is ever new! If we are honest, one of the greatest struggles we share in the Christian life is that of cultivating and maintaining a healthy prayer life. Our great need, therefore, is to echo the disciples' plea to their Master, 'Lord, teach us to pray!' That plea and Christ's answer are taken up in the pages of this book in a way which sees the Lord's Prayer as a pattern for all prayer as much as one which is prescribed for special use. The exposition it contains can only thrill and inspire us afresh to make far more use of the extraordinary privilege of coming to God in prayer.

MARK G. JOHNSTON,
Grove Chapel, Camberwell

Professor Thomas has given us an insightful and inspiring look at the Lord's Prayer. The church has always returned to Christ's instruction on prayer to form prayers that are pleasing to God. In our day when new forms of spirit-uality are appearing all around us, we need to return to this prayer once again. Derek brings us back to this endless source of instruction on prayer in contemporary and practical ways.

RICHARD L. PRATT, JR.,
Third Millenium Ministries

If you would learn to pray, or strengthen your prayer life, who better to instruct you than Jesus. That is why Praying the Saviour's Way can be such a great help to you. The master model for prayer is clearly explained with helpful application.

LUDER WHITLOCK, PRESIDENT EMERITUS,
Reformed Theological Seminary

A splendid book offering fresh insight into the prayer that most Christians know by heart (and often recite without realising and appreciating its vastness and implications). Thomas' teaching has enhanced and deepened my understanding of 'the Lord's Prayer' and made it more precious to me. It has also challenged me about my own prayer life. Too often our prayers are concerned with ourselves and lack the reverence which is due. A misreading of the invitation to call God 'Abba' can lead to an attitude of blatant self-confidence. Rather than being elevated as the most holy 'Father in heaven', God is thus reduced to a Santa Claus-like daddy-God. Thomas writes with knowledge and competence, I find him an inspiring Bible expositor. He shows himself a man of God who has not lost the wonder of being allowed to enter into the presence of the Holy God. As Thomas walks through the 'Lord's Prayer' with us, we discover fundamental truths about both God and ourselves. This book is a powerful reminder of who God is, who we are and what prayer is about.

ELEONORE VAN HAAFTEN,
international author/speaker,
the Netherlands

$\mathcal{P}$raying
the $\mathcal{S}$aviour's $\mathcal{W}$ay

Let Jesus' Prayer Reshape Your Prayer Life

DEREK THOMAS

CHRISTIAN
FOCUS

Derek Thomas is the John E. Richards Professor of Systematic and Practical Theology at Reformed Theological Seminary, Jackson, Mississippi. In addition to his work at the seminary, he serves as the Minister of Teaching at First Presbyterian Church in Jackson.

© Derek Thomas 2001

ISBN 978-1-84550-436-6

10 9 8 7 6 5 4 3 2 1

Published in 2001
with ISBN 1-85792-696-X
Reprinted 2003, 2009
by
Christian Focus Publications Ltd.,
Geanies House, Fearn, Ross-shire,
IV20 1TW, Scotland, Great Britain

www.christianfocus.com

Cover design by Daniel Van Straaten
Printed by Norhaven A/S, Denmark

Contents

To
Bill and Lou Anne

Friends on the other side of the pond!

PREFACE

McCheyne's words (often cited) haunt me: if you want to humble Christians, ask about their prayer lives!

Most of us feel exposed by the poverty of our praying. We talk about a 'prayer life' but there is often precious little *life* about it. We struggle from one aid to another, bothered by the fact that we find it so hard to *grow* in our praying.

Some Christians resent analysis of prayer, as though some sacred ground is violated when we begin to dissect prayer under a spiritual microscope. We may comment about Christian books, or sermons, or Bible studies, but *not* prayer.

Apparently, the disciples found prayer difficult, too. They did not balk at asking Jesus for help. They had heard him pray and wanted to pray like him. Jesus' response? The so-called, *Lord's Prayer*. It is the Bible's 'How to' aid in discipling Christians who are struggling with prayer.

For this reason, *Praying the Saviour's Way* is an exposition of the Lord's Prayer designed to help Christians of all sorts in learning the principles of prayer. Every year, the golfer Jack Nicklaus is reputed to go to his golfing coach and say to him, 'Teach me how to play golf!' So it is with all the Christian disciplines. Sometimes we need to go back to the very foundations and say: 'Teach me to pray!'

I send this book out nervously for fear that anyone who writes a book on prayer might be considered 'an expert'. That would be a mistake because I have to confess that sometimes I feel like an utter novice in prayer. I am, however, persuaded that in this model prayer, the basis for all true prayer is contained. My longing is that what is written here be used to help you grow in the grace of prayer.

Derek W. H. Thomas,
Reformed Theological Seminary
Jackson, Mississippi

1

'Pray ... In This Way'

'Pray, then, in this way...' (Matt. 6:9)

I t may seem a little surprising, even disturbing, that the Christian church has disagreed over these five words; but, it has!

This disagreement has raised some interesting questions. For example, what is the propriety of using the Lord's Prayer in public worship? The *Didache*, for example, a short anonymous book of instruction from the early second century (and possibly late first century), a copy of which did not come to light until the nineteenth century, and whose canonicity was disputed for a while until finally discounted when the canon was fully recognized (at the Council of Carthage in A.D. 397, for example), prescribes that Christians should repeat this prayer three times a day. Though this was a prescription for private, rather than public worship, some of the Church Fathers, Tertullian and Cyprian, for example, commended the Lord's Prayer in particular for use in public worship. Cyprian adds by way of force the incentive: 'What prayer can have greater power with the Father than that which came from the lips of the Son…?' Interestingly, however, the New Testament itself contains no reference to its use in the early church, despite the fact that it reflects the form and structure of the most well-known prayer of synagogue worship, the *Amida* or *Eighteen Benedictions*.

During the Reformation period, John Calvin's liturgy in Geneva also included the Lord's Prayer. Interestingly, it came *after* the sermon along with the Pastoral, or *Great Prayer*. John Knox in Scotland also adopted this use of the Lord's Prayer in his liturgy of 1556. The Book of Common Prayer (1552), under the oversight of Edward VI, brought many changes into the earlier Anglican Prayer Book, removing many of the ceremonies on the advice of many of the Continental Reformers. The service of Morning Prayer included the use of the Lord's Prayer at the point where we are most familiar with it: *before the sermon*.

During the time of the Westminster Assembly, for example, one of the issues that divided the Assembly was the use of the Lord's Prayer in public worship. Presbyterians adopted a view of worship that essentially differed from the Anglicans. The Anglicans (and the Lutherans) said that anything was allowable in worship so long as Scripture didn't expressly forbid it. The Presbyterians, on the other hand, adopted a much stricter view, saying in effect that there would have to be specific warrant for everything that is done in worship. This latter view became known as *the regulative principle* of worship.

The Westminster Assembly, in addition to producing the *Westminster Confession of Faith* with its *Larger* and *Shorter Catechisms* also produced *The Westminster Directory for the Publique Worship of God* (1644). This document was intended to replace the Book of Common Prayer on the grounds that it was too rigid – in not allowing any extemporary prayer, for example. Equally, however, the Westminster Assembly was a gathering of Puritans for whom the issue of *conscience* was very important. Was it right, for example, to insist on a detailed form of worship which the Bible itself has not speci-fically laid down? The kind of enforced uniformity envisioned by the Prayer Book flew in the face of conscience, the Puritans thought. Consequently, they published, not a 'prayer book' implying a rigidly enforced liturgy, but a *Directory* which *recommends* certain practices. It is very important to realize that although the authors of the *Directory* were motivated at every step by the *regulative principle*, they did not envision that all worship services would be uniform. There is a degree of flexibility envisioned within strict observance to the *regulative principle*.

Of interest here is the fact that the *Directory* recommends the use of the Lord's Prayer in worship, saying: 'And because the prayer which Christ taught his disciples is not only a pattern of prayer, but itself a most comprehensive prayer, we recommend it also to be used in the prayers of the Church.'

Later Puritans were to be ambivalent over this recommendation. John Owen, for example, was to write in strong terms against the use of the Lord's Prayer, adding that the fact that this prayer was given by Christ does not imply that we may compose similar prayers as forms for the church's use. Constant repetition, they argued, infringed upon a clear rubric of Christ's regarding the impropriety of *meaningless repetitions* (Matt. 6:7). In addition, the fact that the prayer is given in the context of instruction about 'secret' prayer, rather than public prayer, was sufficient warrant to think that the Lord's Prayer was never designed for constant use in public worship (Matt. 6:6). For many Puritans, the issue of conscience (binding Christians to a form that has not been specifically prescribed) was the fundamental reason why the use of the Lord's Prayer disappeared from the nonconformist churches.

A Pattern

What has all of this taught us? Two things: that the Lord's Prayer is a form which, *occasionally*, is a valid part of public worship; and, that the Lord's Prayer is a form which is *always* instructive when used in either public or private worship. It is this latter feature that is brought out by the words with which Jesus introduces the prayer: 'Pray, then, in this way...' (Matt. 6:9). It is meant to function as a pattern to instruct us on how we should pray. 'Pray...*in this way*...,' using this as a grid by which to measure our own prayers.

What this focuses upon is the fact that many Christians find it difficult to know *what to say* in prayer. Some, of course, think it an interference to analyse prayer. That is a denial of their liberty, and what is thought to be 'the liberty of the Spirit' in prayer. I can recall challenging an individual after a prayer meeting on something he had said during his prayer that seemed particularly offensive, only to be told in no uncertain terms that I had offended the Holy Spirit in doing so! Whilst such folk exist, they are, thankfully, in the minority. Most Christians are far less sure of their utterances. They experience in prayer what is common to every aspect of spirituality: an unrelenting opposition in which we find ourselves battling for survival against a hostile foe. What folk like the Reformer John Calvin, or the Puritan John Owen, or the Anglican bishop J. C. Ryle all witnessed to was that we live our lives in the period known as the 'last days' in a context of spiritual warfare: inwardly against the flesh (Rom. 7:14-25; Gal. 5:16-24), outwardly against the world (Rom. 12:1-2; 1 John 2:15-17), and in both against the devil (1 Pet. 5:8; Eph. 6:10-20). This is why prayer is part of the spiritual fight of faith: the devil knows its value and will do everything within his power to make you either prayerless, or if he cannot accomplish that, as ineffective as possible. And one of the ways he accomplishes the latter is by making us think that because our praying is immature and lacking in depth, the sooner we stop doing it the better.

But this is false reasoning. The answer to immaturity is *growth*. What we need to do is to grow in our praying, just as we are to grow in every aspect of our spiritual lives. By giving us a pattern to follow, Jesus intends that by constant reflection and interaction we might develop a prayer language that is just like it.

The Bible is full of models for prayer. One thinks of the prayers of Abraham, or Ezra, or Nehemiah, or Daniel, or Paul. J. I. Packer has written: 'I believe that prayer is the spiritual measure of men and women in a way that nothing else is, so that how we pray is as important a question as we can ever face.'[1] Indeed, so important is this question of *how* we pray, that such ministers as Matthew Henry[2] and Isaac Watts[3] felt the need to publish volumes designed to help us pray along biblical lines of thought *and* expression.

Then, there are the psalms! One hundred and fifty models of prayer expressing the inner tensions and desires of various psalmists as they brought their hearts to God in prayer. We are meant to pray them. They serve as guides for us to intercede with God. Some of their language and thought world is strange to us; somehow we find it hard to get into them; but, as the seventeenth century minister, Thomas Fuller, put it, the psalms are like clothes parents sometimes purchase for their children, several sizes too big in the hope that they will grow into them.

Balance

Making God the focus of our praying sounds almost too banal to mention; but experience dictates that many Christians have failed to grasp this point. Focusing instead on what God *does*, rather than on who God *is*, redirects the focus of prayer and results in forms of expression that are less honouring than they should be.

What does the pattern of the Lord's Prayer reveal? Several things:

- the prayer consists of a preface followed by six petitions;

- the first three petitions are focused upon God, whilst the last three are directed at man;

- the prayer worships first before it asks for something personal;

- it is comprehensive (covering such things as worship, the kingdom of God, sustenance, grace and protection);

- it embodies three of the four elements of prayer, that is, adoration, petition, and confession (the other being thanksgiving);

- it is brief!

This analysis alone will repay investigation, for we need to ask of our prayers: are they worshipful? Are they God-centred? Are they focused on the kingdom of God? Are they humble and not presumptive? Do they reveal an increasing sense of our depravity? Is their chief end to glorify God? Such questions can help us identify the quality of our praying.

One of the startling things that such analysis can do is to reveal the sheer selfishness of much of our praying. It was Calvin who suggested in his *Institutes of the Christian Religion* that man's mind is a perpetual factory of idols. Idolatry is just the Bible's word for robbing God of his glory, of putting man (ourselves!) at the very centre of things all the time. We don't need to create images or statues to do that; we simply need to ignore that God is there and desires that we worship him. How many prayers become a series of medical reports? Not that such prayers are wrong; far from it! But without the accompanying worship, they become self-centred in a way that is unhealthy; indeed, the very sickness which solicits the prayer may well have been sent to make us focus on the Sender; that in our frailty we might acknowledge his sovereign purposes and worship him accordingly. Some graces grow best in winter, wrote Samuel Rutherford, and some prayers mature when life is bitter. Just as Martin Luther could say of the humanist Erasmus in the days of the Reformation that his god was 'too small', so in our praying, God becomes almost insignificant. He is relegated to the role of a powerful Healer brought in because all else has failed.

When the Athanasian Creed, in its five-minute long exposition of the nature of God, speaks at one point of 'the Father incomprehensible: the Son incomprehensible: and the Holy Ghost incompre-hensible:...' [*Immensus Pater: immensus Filius: immensus Spiritus Sanctus*], its design was to extol the unimaginable greatness of the Triune God of Scripture. Whilst our prayers may not be able to reflect the precision of the Athanasian Creed (!), their general aim in exalting God ought to be evident. Far too often, we rush into intercession, asking for God's help in this or that, without first basking in the fact that we can address him at all!

Simplicity

There is something disarmingly *simple* about the Lord's Prayer. Of course, when we look at it closely it turns out to be much deeper than we think; nevertheless, its form is essentially straightforward and undemanding. Three features emerge:

1. Prayer is *conversational* response. It is conversational in nature as though we were answering questions put to

us by God. Questions like: *Who do you think I am?* ('Our Father, who art in heaven'). *What is it that you desire most?* ('To hallow your Name'). *What else do you desire?* ('...daily bread...forgiveness...guidance along the way').

2. Prayer is *covenantal*: it expresses our relationship to God and his relationship to us. 'I will be your God and you shall be my people' is a refrain that echoes the covenant bond throughout the Bible (Exod. 6:7; Jer. 7:23; 11:4; 30:22; Ezek. 36:28; 2 Cor. 6:16; Heb. 8:10). The Lord's Prayer echoes this fellowship. There is nothing in this prayer that a child could not pray. Of course, we shall understand its petitions to greater depths, but the point is that the language the Lord has chosen here is reflective of the intimacy that we all enjoy with our heavenly Father. Because we know him, and not simply that we know *about* him, we can pray like this.

Jesus rebuked the lengthy discourses of the Pharisees as well as the mindless repetitions of pagans. The Lord's Prayer is to be our model. Praying 'like this' is sufficient to gain the ear of the Almighty God. Its structure is meant to ensure that we *think about* what we pray. Its balance is meant to ensure that we place God first. Its simplicity is meant to encourage every believer to be a prayer-warrior.

3. Prayer is about *consistency*. It is to our private devotions that Jesus calls attention by way of a prelude to this prayer. What enables prayer is the constant resort to what Jesus calls in this passage, 'secret' prayer (Matt. 6:6). It is a lesson that emerges in Scripture in more than one location, that what we are in private is determinative of what we may become in public. In the wonderful 'model' prayer of Daniel in Daniel 9:4-19, the eloquence is breathtaking. We read the prayer and long to be able to pray like that! But the secret to Daniel's public prayer lay in his habitual resort to prayer as the paradigm by which he lived his entire life. The Key to Daniel's extraordinary outpouring lies in what we read earlier:

'Now when Daniel knew that the document was signed, he entered his house (now in his roof chamber he had windows open toward Jerusalem); and he continued kneeling on his knees three times a day, praying and giving thanks before his God, as he had been doing previously' (Dan. 6:10). Daniel had a personal commitment to prayer in the secret place. He reached the height because he was always climbing. For almost seventy years, this had been the pattern of his life.

Similarly, it is a resolve to be men and women of prayer in the ordinary course of life that enables us to be men and women of prayer in the extraordinary occasions.

'Lord, teach us to pray...in secret, as well as in public.'

2

OUR FATHER

J esus did not pray the Lord's Prayer himself. The petition for forgiveness would not have been appro-priate for him to pray since he was without sin.

The church has called this prayer *The Lord's Prayer* because this is the prayer he taught his disciples to pray. It is the prayer of those who are living the life of the kingdom of God and doing so in the presence of their heavenly Father. In it, Jesus gives the fundamental structure and order of things for which we are to pray. But the prayer also teaches us how he expects us to live the Christian life in fellowship with God. Jesus tells us what life in fellowship with God is like in the New Covenant.

If we were to ask for those principles by which all Christians ought to live their lives from the point of view of the teaching of the New Testament, we could very simply point to the Lord's Prayer. Even though this is a prayer, couched in terms of adoration, confession and petition, it is *also* a compendium of theology; it is a teaching tool, a catechism summarizing those things we are bound to know if we are to make progress in the kingdom of God. We can usefully gauge our theology as well as our praying by the standards of this prayer.

The *preface* (as it is called) to the Lord's Prayer, 'Our Father in heaven' (Matt. 6:9), is perhaps the most spiritually determinative of our spiritual condition. Repeating these words can signify what is most essential for us: an appreciation that the God of heaven is our Father. In a most profound sense, theologians have noted that to be able to call God, 'Father,' is what the message of the New Testament is principally about.

J. I. Packer wrote some time ago that 'You sum up the whole of the New Testament teaching in a single phrase, if you speak of it as a revelation of the Fatherhood of the holy Creator.'[4] Similarly, Sinclair Ferguson has written: 'You cannot open the pages of the New Testament without realizing that one of the things that makes it so "new", in every way, is that here men and women call God "Father".'[5] The Fatherhood of God, or its corollary, our sonship or adoption, is the very heartbeat of the new covenant. A failure to appreciate this can be fatal. If we never know what it is to commune with God as our Father, we fail to grasp the meaning of what Jesus Christ accomplished for us.

God's Fatherhood

Reading through the Bible in a cursory fashion will reveal that the designation, 'Father,' is used of God in both the Old Testament and the New Testament. But he is not called 'Father' in precisely the same sense everywhere in the Bible.

Sometimes the term reflects the fact that he is the Creator of the universe in which we live. Malachi, for example, asks the question: 'Have we not all one Father? Did not one God create us?' (Mal. 2:10). And even in the New Testament there is a sense in which Paul can agree that we are all 'his offspring' in the sense that we are all created by God (Acts 17:28). God is 'the Father of the heavenly lights,' in the sense that he is the Creator of every star in the night sky (James 1:17).

Of greater significance, however, is the fact that this is the way Jesus thought about his own relationship to God. It is with the expression 'Father' that Jesus addresses God. Six times, for example, he calls upon his Father in heaven in the so-called High Priestly Prayer of John 17 (vv. 1, 5, 11, 21, 24, 25). In a sense, it might be better if we had called John 17 *The Lord's Prayer*, and The Lord's Prayer, *The Disciples' Prayer*! Something of the inner soul of Jesus is revealed in this prayer in John 17. Perhaps this is why John Knox, as he was dying, asked for this chapter to be read to him. Jesus and his disciples share a common rela-tionship with God; both refer to him as 'Father'.

This is brought out in the words Jesus spoke to Mary Magdalene on the morning of the resurrection. As she clung to him, he said, 'Do not hold on to me, for I have not yet returned to the Father. Go instead to my brothers and tell them, "I am returning to my Father and your Father, to my God and your God"' (John 20:17). It is often thought that these words illustrate the fact that Jesus' relationship to his Father is *different* from ours. He is, after all, the *eternal Son* of God, and we become sons by adoption. But whilst there is an aspect of this which is true, the point of this incident is the very opposite: it is to signal that his ascension will inaugurate a similar relationship with God that he has enjoyed, and hence he tells Mary, 'Go…to my *brothers* and tell them…' Jesus is our Elder Brother in a relationship in which God is our Father. Jesus' personal gift to those who trust in him is this: 'You can call him "Father" too!' It is as though Jesus is saying, 'You will be able to call on God in the same way that you have heard me do for these past few years.'

Nothing encourages prayer more than the realization that we have this relationship with God by which we call him, 'Father.' In comparison with Old Testament believers, burdened by ceremonial restrictions of access, the fact that we can come to God in this way is breathtaking. A new order of reality has dawned with the coming of a new covenant in which 'because you are sons, God sent the Spirit of his Son into our hearts, the Spirit who calls out, "Abba, Father." So you are no longer a slave, but a son' (Gal. 4:6-7). Christians belong to that Jerusalem which is above which is free (Gal. 4:26).

We dare to call him '*Our* Father.'

Knowing God

It is one thing to know this truth in an intellectual sense; but it is another to know it experientially. And it is one of those self-revealing things about a person that in a moment of crisis and difficulty, they have recourse to a Father who loves them and cares for them. What so many folk do in a crisis, and you hear it all the time, is to mouth the name 'Jesus' only because they have used it as a swear word so many times. But now, in a crisis, when they feel they need help, they can only say 'Jesus' without comprehension of what a believer in Jesus can know. It is interesting to note that many men do not instinctively cry out, 'O Father!' because they do not know him as a Father. If you don't have the heart of a child, the instinct to call him 'Father' is not there.

John's Gospel does not only begin with a magnificent word about Jesus as the Word of God (John 1:1), it also has something to say about how we may come to know him as Saviour and Lord: 'Yet to all who received him, to those who believed in his name, he gave the right to become children of God' (John 1:12). Reborn by the power of God, they are given the right to call God their heavenly Father. Having come to new life through regeneration, we are received into a new family – *God's* family! With the transformation of our nature, we are introduced into a new relationship.

Those who have legally adopted children can relate to that moment whenever a child first begins instinctively to say 'Daddy' or 'Mammy'. No explanation of the legal process can do justice to the sound of those words. And what God desires most of all is that his children not only possess the legal right to the privileges of adoption, but that they have a nature that can respond to them in words that betray the intimacy and closeness of their new relationship. Instinctively, they say, 'Abba, Father' (Rom. 8:15; Gal. 4:6). The new nature gives rise to new instincts: so that in trouble we instinctively say, 'My Father in heaven.'

It was a singular emphasis in John Calvin, for example, that the very essence of piety lies in the recognition that our lives are nourished by God's Fatherly care. That is why, Calvin adds, the 'first title' given to the Holy Spirit in the New Testament is 'Spirit of adoption'.[6] As one eminent scholar has summed it up: 'It is the knowledge of his Fatherly love that is the true knowledge of God.'[7] The late New Testament scholar, Joachim Jeremias, has pointed out that the church's use of the term 'Abba' to denote God the Father was a repetition of the way they had heard Jesus address his Father in heaven. (cf. Mark 14:36 with Rom. 8:15 and Gal. 4:6).[8] What the truth of Fatherhood through regeneration and adoption means experientially is this: *we are loved by God no less than Jesus was loved by God.* As startling as that sounds, it is true! We, like Jesus, come before our God and call him, 'Abba, Father.'

What this emphasis in the New Testament points to is that the early Christians were imitating some-thing they had heard Jesus say. They were praying like him! The writer of Hebrews can say, 'Jesus is not ashamed to call them brothers' (Heb. 2:11). This, by the way, is the short-sightedness of those who claim that there is nothing of Christ in this prayer.

27

Whilst it is true that generally we should address the Father, through the Son's mediation, and by the help of the Spirit, this does not mean that it is never right to address Jesus or the Holy Spirit directly in prayer. But the norm is as here: we talk to our Father in heaven. But in doing so, we are reminded of our relationship to Jesus Christ. We pray like he prayed! As Calvin points out in his eloquent exposition of the Lord's Prayer in the *Institutes*:

> He, while he is the true Son, has of himself been
> given us as a brother that what he has of his own
> nature may become ours by benefit of adoption if
> we embrace this great blessing with sure faith.[9]

It is the unexpectedness of this Fatherly love to which John gives testimony in his first epistle: 'How great is the love the Father has lavished on us, that we should be called children of God! And that is what we are!' (1 John 3:1). The translation here obscures something that John says. Literally, he says, 'What *manner* of love…', using a word that refers to quality: what *kind* of love is this? It is as though he were saying, 'God's love *is out of this world…*'

What is to the fore here is our access to the Father. Jesus refers to two different and paralysing conditions of the human heart: hypocrisy and anxiety. These are very different problems, but Jesus tells us in the sections which precede and follow the Lord's Prayer in Matthew's Gospel that in essence they have the same solution. To both hypocrites (Matt. 6:1-4) and the anxious (Matt. 7:25-34), Jesus says that the problem is that they do not know God as their heavenly Father. The hypocrytes would not need to try and impress others with outward show if they knew God as their Father in heaven. Similarly, the anxious are betraying a lack of trust in the Father's provision. The problems are very different, but the solution is the same.

It is the same problem that bedevils us all: that we do not live as those who have a heavenly Father who takes care of our every need. It is to this that Paul speaks in Romans 8 at great length. Speaking of the 'weaknesses' which every Christian knows, Paul goes on to address the problem this creates, by saying: 'We do not know what we ought to pray for, but the Spirit himself intercedes for us with groans that words cannot express' (Rom. 8:26). We pray in our weakness with the Spirit's help. Earlier in the chapter, Paul refers to the Spirit again in the context of prayer and access to God, saying that it is by his help that we can call God, 'Abba, Father' (Rom. 8:15). What is not often appreciated is that this cry arises in the context of weakness and unbelief. It is because we are weak and suffering, troubled by a thousand cares, that the Spirit helps us cry. The word 'cry' which Paul uses is used elsewhere of the agonized cries of those in distress (e.g. Matt. 15:22; Mark 3:11). In our most troubled times, we have access, by the Spirit's help, to God as our Father. That is the encouragement held out to us. At our very lowest, when there is nothing else left, our deepest instinct is to say, 'O Father!' And we have the assurance, 'He who did not spare his own Son, but gave him up for us all – how will he not also, along with him, graciously give us all things?' (Rom. 8:32).

Heaven

There have been attempts to place this New Testament emphasis upon sonship in the foreground and thereby re-dress what has appeared to some as the imbalance of those Christians whose outlook is related too exclusively to the eternal future. The *Sonship* program, for example, popular in the United States, attempts to do that and for those recovering from fundamentalist legalism, its attraction is understandable.[10]

There are some presentations of what is perceived to be the New Testament emphasis on adoption that carry an agenda that is decidedly unbiblical. In attempting to emphasize our access to God and the intimacy of our relationship, denials can very easily creep in as to issues of reverence and submission. Liberty can easily give way to license. Access can become presumptuous and over-familiar. The term 'Abba,' for example, can be thought to convey what we might refer to as 'Daddy' or 'Pops'.

That is why the Lord's Prayer provides for us a corrective by saying, 'Our Father *in heaven*.' 'By this,' Calvin writes, God 'is lifted up above all chance of either corruption or change…it is as if he had been said to be of infinite greatness or loftiness, of incomprehensible essence, of bound-less might, and of everlasting immortality.'[11] This, together with the first petition to 'hallow' God's name, reminds us that we are always to be reverent in God's presence. We come as children, but with humility. Meekness must always mark the children of God (Matt. 5:5).

The balancing of these twin truths keeps our feet on the ground and our heads from swelling. We think of our Father and yet remind ourselves that he dwells 'in unapproachable light' (1 Tim. 6:16). We think of God's greatness and majesty and call him, 'Father.'

Something else is in view here. By adding 'in heaven' Jesus wants us to understand that the one who most desires to help us is *able* to do so. Because he resides in heaven he is in a position to do for us what we cannot do. 'His almighty arm,' writes Witsius, 'which is ever ready to be stretched forth in behalf of his own people, no created power is able to resist.'[12] It is this reassurance of divine aid that draws us into this prayer. We long to make it our own. We are helpless creatures in need of such aid as our Father is more than able to provide.

Whate'er my God ordains is right:
   Here shall my stand be taken;
Though sorrow, need, or death be mine,
   Yet am I not forsaken.
    My Father's care
    Is round me there;
He holds me that I shall not fall;
And so to Him I leave it all.

                  Samuel Rodigast (1649-1708).

This is our encouragement to pray with confidence.

3

REVERENCE

*E*ven a cursory reading of the Bible will reveal that names are important to the biblical writers. Names are significant, and none more so than the names of God.

Names of God

God has several names in the Bible. Two stand out above the rest. The first and most basic is the name *El*, or *Eloah*, or *Elohim*. All of these are usually translated as 'God' in our English Bibles. There are also some well-known compound forms, including *El Shaddai*, as well as names of individuals in which the root '*el* can be seen, as in Elijah, Elisha and Ishmael.

The meaning of words can sometimes be ascertained by looking at the roots of words and seeing how they developed. Surprisingly, there isn't much agreement amongst scholars as to the root of these words, but most seem to think that the most basic form is *Eloah*, partly because its most frequent occurrence is in those passages which are amongst the oldest in Scripture (it occurs over forty times in Job for example).

In Deuteronomy 32, the Song of Moses celebrating their deliverance from Egypt and anticipation of Canaan, the word occurs in parallel with 'Rock' (Deut. 32:15). The meaning of *Eloah* has to do with strength and power. God is a great power. That would explain why it is this group of words, specifically *Elohim*, that is used in the opening sentences of the Bible about how God created the heavens and the earth.

The use of 'us' and 'our' in the creation account does appear to allude to something which only later in the Bible becomes clear: that God is one and God is more than one. Even in the very first chapter, the Hebrew (and no other Semitic language does this) introduces us to God as though it were saying, 'There is more to him than you imagine.' Some writers have suggested that since *Elohim* is in the plural, the word provides an early reference to the Trinity. On the other hand, liberals of the last century suggested the plural was proof that the Jewish religion developed (evolved) from a more primitive one in which polytheism was the norm, but the evidence for this is non-existent. Others have suggested that what is in view is the 'plural of majesty'.

Yahweh

God has another specific designation, one which he gave to the church and by which he demands to be called. It is the name *Jehovah*, or as it is now increasingly vocalized, *Yahweh*. In our English Bibles it is usually capitalized as 'LORD'. The name is first given in Exodus 3, where Moses is being commissioned to return to Egypt as God's emissary in the deliverance of Israel from slavery. Moses expresses his reluctance, suggesting that he would need to know what name he should use to describe the God who is to deliver them. This time, God tells him that his name is 'I AM WHO I AM. This is what you are to say to the Israelites: "I AM has sent me to you"' (Exod. 3:14). In the very next verse, God goes on to say to Moses: 'Say to the Israelites, "The LORD, the

God of your fathers— the God of Abraham, the God of Isaac and the God of Jacob— has sent me to you."This is my name for ever, the name by which I am to be remembered from generation to generation' (Exod. 3:15). The Hebrew for LORD sounds like and may be derived from the Hebrew for I AM in verse 14. God is the LORD, the I AM. It is also possible that the tense should be future rather than the present, in which case Moses is being told that God's name, LORD, is 'I WILL BE.'

The Jews thought the name LORD (*Yahweh*) was so holy that they refused to vocalize it and instead used a title made up of the vowels for another name of God, *Adonai* (which is often translated 'Lord' in lower case), along with the consonants of *Yahweh*. Hebrew was written in earlier times without vowels, and this made the substitution all the more easy to perform. It is not at all certain that we have the correct pronunciation of *Yahweh*, and this has led some to be cautious in its use.[13]

But where has all this brought us? The LORD is the 'I AM,' signifying his eternal existence. Theologians have talked about the *aseity* of God, by which they have meant God's eternal or independent existence. He owes his existence to no one. He is the uncreated being. Everyone, everything else, has an origin, but God is absolutely independent. The bush that was on fire, and yet was not consumed, spoke of the God who 'did not burn up' (Exod. 3:2).

But, the name 'I AM THAT I AM' (or I WILL BE WHAT I WILL BE) is more significant than simply a statement of God's eternal and independent existence. As Exodus 3:15 shows, the name LORD is closely associated with the relationship God had with Abraham, Isaac and Jacob. It is his *covenant* name. It is the name in which he bonds with his people. It is interesting that in verse 12, God says to Moses 'I will be with you.' The One who signifies that he is the 'I AM,' or 'I WILL BE,' also says that he is the One who 'WILL BE WITH US.' That would make sense: the

God who is transcendent is also immanent. He is 'high and exalted' and yet he is in the midst of his people (cf. Isa. 6:1).

It is deeply interesting that the New Testament pours into the name *Yahweh* an even deeper significance. John, for example, in the last book of the Bible, speaks of Christ using a formula derived from the Greek translation of the Hebrew Scriptures of Exodus 3:14, referring to him as 'him who is, and who was, and who is to come... the Alpha and the Omega...who is, and who was, and who is to come, the Almighty' (Rev. 1:4, 8). The book of Revelation is saying – with such clarity: Jesus is *Yahweh*! The God of the Old Testament is Jesus Christ.

What has all this to do with the Lord's Prayer? Quite simply, that the first petition calls for us to think about God, and in particular his Name. Our prayers are to be suffused with large thoughts about God. We are to take the attributes of God which are suggested by his various names. If our prayers are not focused on God we are guilty of idolatry; we are putting someone (or something) else in God's place.

We are not to think of God in any other way but that way in which he has revealed himself. Calvin, citing Hilary of Poitiers (c. 315–365) in his work *On the Trinity*, wrote: 'God alone is a fit witness of himself in his Word.'[14] We are to take everything God has disclosed about himself in the Word and turn it into prayer. It is a mark of the worldliness of our praying that we are far too little occupied with God when we pray. Too often, we rush into intercession without pausing to reflect on the character of the God we are addressing. Taking time to pause and reflect on God's being is what the Lord's Prayer beckons us to do. Let us not then be in a hurry when we address the Almighty!

A holy God

'Hallowed be Your name ...' But what does 'hallowed' mean? After all, it is not a word we use in our everyday speech.

One modern translation puts it this way: 'May your name be honored.'[15] Eugene Peterson in his free translation of the New Testament renders it, 'Reveal who you are.'[16]

The Greek word translated 'hallowed' is the verb form of the word for 'holy'. We do not have a verb form in the English language and hence we say 'sanctify', not 'holify'. The word is the usual one in the New Testament for sanctification. From its Old Testament usage in particular, 'sanctify' has the basic idea of 'setting apart'. It is what Peter says: 'set apart Christ as Lord' (1 Pet. 3:15). It is what Isaiah says:

> The LORD Almighty is the one you are to regard
> as holy,
>> he is the one you are to fear,
>> he is the one you are to dread (Isa. 8:13).

God is to be revered. He is to be thought of, and spoken about, and served with godly fear. He is to be set apart, not in the sense of placed on a shelf and then ignored, but in the sense of being exalted above everything (everyone) else and worshipped. In our theology it means having great thoughts of God – think of what B. B. Warfield called Reformed Theology, 'a profound apprehension of God in majesty.' In prayer it means spending some time cleansing our minds of the dirt that soils and filling our thoughts with God's incomprehensible greatness and majesty. In speech it means using words that describe him in ways that extol him.

Sanctifying God! It almost sounds heretical, doesn't it! And it would be if, by this expression, we meant that God can be made more holy and majestic than he is. But that is not what we mean when we say: 'Hallowed be Thy name.' It is not that God is made more holy than he is, but that he is more holy than we have imagined him to be. We are to pray that he will become *more* glorious in our eyes.

There is a purposeful balance in the Lord's Prayer between God's immanence and transcendence, his nearness to us and distance from us. Some theological systems fail to appreciate that. Some, for example, in the interests of maintaining our relationship to him as children, suggest that it is never right to be motivated by fear, but that we should always be motivated by love. But this is far too simplistic a distinction to draw. The book of Hebrews, for example, could not be more explicit: 'Therefore, since we are receiving a kingdom that cannot be shaken, let us be thankful, and so worship God acceptably with reverence and awe, for our "God is a consuming fire"'(Heb. 12:28-29). And Peter can say: 'Since you call on a Father who judges each man's work impartially, live your lives as strangers here in reverent fear' (1 Pet. 1:17).

Reverent fear! According to one dictionary of theology, commenting in this case on the Old Testament, 'The fear of God is the decisive religious factor in Old Testament piety.'[17] Another, with the entire Bible in mind, puts it this way: 'True religion is often synonymous with the fear of God.'[18] The Lord's Prayer urges us to reverence God. We are to fear him. Is it ever right to be afraid of God? The question needs to be handled very carefully, but it is the height of folly, as John Murray argues, not to be afraid of God when there is every reason to be afraid.[19] To any professing Christian who begins to think in terms that lie outside of Scripture's ethical norm, there is every reason to be afraid. To the sincere Christian who is trying to walk within the terms of covenant life, there is no cause to be afraid, but there is every reason to revere. Did not Jesus say: 'Do not be afraid of those who kill the body but cannot kill the soul. Rather, be afraid of the One who can destroy both soul and body in hell' (Matt. 10:28). 'My flesh trembles for fear of Thee, And I am afraid of Thy judgments' (Ps. 119:120, NASB). There are times when it is right to tremble!

Fearing God brings wisdom and knowledge:

'The fear of the LORD is the beginning of knowledge' (Prov. 1:7).

'The fear of the LORD is the beginning of wisdom' (Prov. 9:10).

'Always be zealous for the fear of the LORD' (Prov. 23:17).

God's holiness and our sin

When God's holiness is perceived, the invariable consequence is that the believer's own unworthiness is exposed. So it was with Isaiah: ' "Woe to me!" I cried' (Isa. 6:5). Thus it was with Peter: 'Go away from me, Lord; I am a sinful man!' (Luke 5:8). Thus it was with John: 'When I saw him, I fell at his feet as though dead' (Rev. 1:17).

This is the way we 'hallow' God's name. As we decrease, he will increase. He cannot be set apart in proud hearts, for there is no room for him. Only empty vessels can he fill.

> His name for ever shall endure;
>   Last like the sun it shall:
> Men shall be blessed in him, and blessed
>   All nations shall him call.
>
> Now blessed be the Lord our God,
>   The God of Israel.
> For he alone doth wondrous works,
>   In glory that excel.
>
> And blessed be his glorious name
>   To all eternity:
> The whole earth let his glory fill.
>   Amen, so let it be
>
> (Ps. 72:17-19, Metrical Version).

4

THE KINGDOM

Those who discover the Lord's Prayer for the first time think that some of its petitions do not say a great deal. This one, for example: 'Thy Kingdom come...' We might be excused for thinking that this is a prayer for missions and leave it at that. In that case, turning to the Larger Catechism will correct us:

> In the second petition, which is, 'Thy kingdom come,' acknowledging ourselves and all mankind to be by nature under the dominion of sin and Satan, we pray, that the kingdom of sin and Satan may be destroyed, the gospel propagated throughout the world, the Jews called, the fullness of the Gentiles brought in; the church furnished with all gospel-officers and ordinances, purged from corruption, countenanced and maintained by the civil magistrate: that the ordinances of Christ may be purely dispensed,

and made effectual to the converting of those
that are yet in their sins, and the confirming,
comforting, and building up of those that are
already converted: that Christ would rule in our
hearts here, and hasten the time of his second
coming, and our reigning with him for ever:
and that he would be pleased so to exercise the
kingdom of his power in all the world, as may
best conduce to these ends.

Reading this profound enlargement of the second petition
of the Lord's Prayer may help us understand why George
Gillespie, one of the Scottish Presbyterian delegates to the
Westminster Assembly, said of the Larger Catechism that it
was 'for those of understanding'. Perhaps; but, reading this
statement carefully will help us appreciate just how full and
profound a prayer the Lord's Prayer is. This petition encap-
sulates the entire purpose of God in the world. Such questions as: Why did Jesus come into the world? What is the
relationship of the Old Testament to the New Testament?
What is the function of the church of Christ? What is God
doing in the world today? – such issues as these are all involved in this petition! We can say, therefore, that this petition is at the heart of the message of the Bible.

Reading the Gospels, particularly the Gospels of Matthew, Mark and Luke, will underline for us how central the
message of *the kingdom of God* was to our Lord Jesus Christ.
Matthew introduces Jesus' public ministry by saying, 'Jesus went throughout Galilee, teaching in their synagogues,
preaching the good news of the kingdom, and healing every
disease and sickness among the people' (Matt. 4:23). If we
were to ask what is central to his message, we could do no
better than to cite Matthew again: 'From that time on Jesus
began to preach, "Repent, for the kingdom of heaven is near"'

(Matt. 4:17). Luke is even more pointed as to the purpose of Jesus' mission: 'I must preach the good news of the kingdom of God to the other towns also, because that is why I was sent' (Luke 4:43). The Sermon on the Mount tells us that Jesus intends his followers to live in his kingdom according to a kingdom pattern, so that the chief goal of every believer is to 'seek first his kingdom and his righteousness' (Matt. 6:33). Luke informs us that during the forty-day period following the resurrection and ascension, Jesus 'spoke about the kingdom of God' (Acts 1:3). Luke further tells us that the early church engaged in something which he describes as preaching 'the good news of the kingdom of God' (Acts 8:12). In Ephesus, Paul spent three months in the synagogue 'arguing persuasively about the kingdom of God' (Acts 19:8), as he did later in Rome (Acts 28:23), Luke adding that for two years 'boldly and without hindrance he preached the kingdom of God and taught about the Lord Jesus Christ' (Acts 28:31).

Ruler

Clearly, the kingdom of God (or the kingdom of heaven) is a major theme in the Bible. Matthew uses the expression 'kingdom of heaven' (over thirty times) rather than 'kingdom of God' because, it seems, he was writing primarily to Jews who had certain misgivings about using the name of God in speech. The expression 'kingdom of God' occurs sixty-five times in the New Testament, primarily in the first three Gospels and Acts. Though both John and Paul use the expression, it is not a favourite of theirs (John 3:3, 5; Gal. 5:21; Col 4:11; 2 Thess. 1:5).

But what does it mean?

Firstly, this petition alludes to the sovereign rule of God as King over the entire universe.

That God is King is a message that appears like bookends in the first and last chapters of the Bible. The Lord who merely speaks all things into existence at the creation is King. His word is authoritative and powerful. He says: 'Let there be' and there is! The nature of the genesis of the universe speaks of a sovereignty that is shared by no lesser being. In the beginning there is God and no one else. Equally, the Bible closes with a glimpse of the new city. At the centre of it – 'the throne of God and of the Lamb will be in the city, and his servants will serve him' (Rev. 22:3). The vision of the future is one in which God rules as King.

However, is it not true to say that the words 'King' and 'kingdom,' or king*ship* and king*dom* mean two quite different things? Yes, partly this is true. 'King*ship*' alludes to God's rule over the entire universe, whilst 'kingdom' is a narrower frame of reference which has to do with how that rule of God is exercised redemptively. The former idea finds its way into the Lord's Prayer in the (it has to be said, *disputed*) assertion that closes it: 'Yours is the *kingdom*' (Matt. 6:13, in most English texts in footnotes). Here, in the second petition, it is the second idea, that of the rule of God in a redemptive sense, that is in view. The two ideas cannot be completely divorced: it is because God rules over everything that he rules over his people in particular.

God reigns over his people in particular! That leads us to another thought: this petition alludes to the covenantal rule of God over his people.

Old Testament

It is interesting to note that the first preacher of the New Testament, not Jesus but John the Baptist as Jesus' forerunner, is introduced in the same way as his Master: he 'came, preaching…"Repent, for the kingdom of heaven is near"' (Matt. 3:1-2). Both John and Jesus, in preaching 'the kingdom of God (heaven),' can assume that their hearers understood what they meant. Neither engage in explanations of its meaning, and that is because their hearers had expected such a message from their understanding of the Old Testament. The popular understanding of the Old Testament must have been that its message was about the kingdom of God.

Interesting? Yes, because the expression 'kingdom of God' is not found in the Old Testament! And only a handful of references to a kingdom that is specifically 'the Lord's' can be found (e.g. Ps. 22:28; 103:22; 114:2; 145:13; Obad. 21). However, if the expression is unknown in the Old Testament, the idea is not. On every page of the Old Testament there is the expectation that God is working out a plan and purpose in which he is gathering a people to himself and over which he intends to exercise his rule. He enters into covenant with his people with the precise agenda that they might be his people, and he will be their God.

Whether it be the covenant with Abraham or Moses or David, there is an expectation that covenant life and privilege will bring covenant responsibilities and character. Indeed, there is a sense in which this kingdom is announced in the Garden of Eden in the *protoevangelium*, the promise that the seed of the woman will crush the head of Satan (Gen. 3:15). This promise is particularized in Abraham when God promises that from his seed would descend a nation that would not only occupy Canaan, but would also be the means by which the nations of the world would find blessing (Gen. 12: 2-3). As you trace the story of the people of God through the pages of the Old Testament, you are in effect tracing the fulfilment of this promise. Not only that, but the history of the New Testament is the fulfilment of that promise too. So much so, that Peter could explain the events of Pentecost and the conversion of thousands of Jews and particularly Gentiles, as none other than the fulfilment of the promise made to Abraham (Acts 3:25). The church of the New Testament is the seed of Abraham: 'If you belong to Christ, then you are Abraham's seed, and heirs according to the promise' (Gal. 3:29).

A divine plan

There were times in the history of the Old Testament when it was difficult to see how God was fulfilling this promise. In the closing chapters of Genesis, for example, Moses is trying to address that very issue when he relates the death of Jacob in the land of Egypt and how Jacob insisted that he be buried in Canaan, in a grave which he himself had dug (Gen. 50:5). The description of the Egyptians' court that accompanied Jacob's body to Canaan, with 'chariots and horsemen' (Gen. 50:9) is designed to indicate this very thing: Moses must have been chuckling as he wrote it, giving us a glimpse of what will later come to pass, that the very nations are coming to Zion. Even through the dire history of Egyptian bondage and slavery, God was working out his purpose. As Joseph said to his brothers, in the face of their malice and hatred of him: 'You intended to harm me, but God intended it for good to accomplish what is now being done, the saving of many lives' (Gen. 50:20).

God always keeps his promises! He intends to gather in his people, no matter how it may appear to us at this moment. God will gather his elect from the corners of the world and bring them to himself for ever. There will come a time when it shall be said: 'The kingdom of the world has become the kingdom of our Lord and of his Christ, and he will reign for ever and ever' (Rev. 11:15).

Thirdly, this petition alludes to God's intention to overthrow all of Satan's pretensions to power.

We have already alluded to Genesis 3:15, and the threat to Satan that it contains. As the Larger Catechism notes, in this petition of the Lord's Prayer we pray, 'that the kingdom of...*Satan* may be destroyed.' It is interesting to note how little this particular feature of the work of Jesus Christ has been highlighted over the centuries, partly in reaction to aberrant views of the atonement by theologians of the medieval age, in which Christ was thought to pay a ransom to the devil. It took a while for theologians to recover from this imbalance and stress the biblical emphasis expressed in such passages as 1 John 3:8: 'The reason the Son of God appeared was to destroy the devil's work.' Or, Colossians 2:15: 'And having disarmed the powers and authorities, he made a public spectacle of them, triumphing over them by the cross.'

Christ, in his resurrection, proclaims his triumph not only over death, but over Satan too. From the moment he began his public ministry, his intention to defeat Satan is announced by the Spirit's (yes, the Spirit's) driving of him into the wilderness to face Satan in three successive assaults. These temptations, whilst they may have something to say to us as we face temptations, must be understood primarily as a declaration of war by Jesus against the forces of darkness. Interesting, too, is the account John gives us of the Upper Room and the words which conclude the fourteenth chapter, where Jesus says to his disciples: 'let us leave' (John 14:31). These words have always proved difficult since they don't actually leave until the end of chapter 17! But this is to misunderstand what Jesus is saying. The words are capable of another rendition, a military one in which Jesus is announcing his intention, not to leave the Upper Room, but to go and face his enemy in battle. In the previous verse, Jesus reassures his disciples by saying: 'I will not speak with you much longer, for the prince of this world is coming. He has no hold on me' (John 14:30). Commenting on a passage in John 16, Calvin could summarize what Jesus is saying in the Upper Room in this way: 'I have therefore resolved to furnish you with the necessary weapons for this warfare.'[20] The Prince of light is preparing to do battle with the prince of darkness. It is not insignificant that Jesus' final words from the cross were: 'It is finished' (John 19:30). In part, at least, Jesus is alluding to his triumph and conquest in the battle he has endured against his most implacable enemy. The Servant of the Lord who came in battle armour has routed his opposition in glorious triumph (Isa. 59:16-17). *Christus Victor*. Christ is Victor!

Kingdom come *and* coming

It will be noticed that the second petition is a prayer and not an assertion. We are to pray for the kingdom, which suggests that the kingdom has not already arrived. But do we not read in the New Testament words which seem to indicate that it has? With allusions to his casting out of demons, Jesus could conclude 'the kingdom of God has come upon you' (Matt. 12:28; Luke 11:20). The Strong Man is bound and the Christ is robbing his house (Matt. 12:29). On another occasion, in the inauguration of the Lord's Supper, he told his disciples: 'I tell you the truth, I will not drink again of the fruit of the vine until that day when I drink it anew in the kingdom of God' (Mark 14:25). The kingdom of God *has* come and the kingdom of God *is yet* to come! How can this be?

This leads us to another point with regard to the kingdom of God:

Fourthly, this petition alludes to the as yet incomplete nature of the kingdom of God.

We live as Christians, you and I, in the time between the two great advents of Christ. The Incarnation is past; the Second Coming is future. We live in the 'last days' (Heb. 1:2). We are those upon whom 'the end of ages' has dawned (1 Pet. 1:20; cf. Heb. 9:26). There is 'now,' but there is also a 'not yet'. The Gadarene demoniacs recognized this and complained: 'What do you want with us, Son of God?' they shouted. 'Have you come here to torture us before the appointed time?'

(Matt. 8:29). But the end is not yet. The decisive battle has been won, but the ultimate victory celebration must await the final triumph of Christ in the establishment of the new heavens and new earth. Satan refuses to believe it is all over and continues to struggle, with death-throes that at times are vicious in character. Hence the church lives in the arena of conflict, and 'times of stress' (2 Tim. 3:1, RSV). It will find expression in the final petition of the Lord's Prayer, 'Deliver us from the evil one' (Matt. 6:13).

In personal terms, this means that although the decisive change has taken place in our regeneration and union with Christ (we are not, nor can ever be, what we once were), the change is incomplete. We are sinners still, and hence we feel the pull of sin that would (if it could) drag us down so as to deny Christ entirely. We wrestle, then, against the world, the flesh and devil. We live our lives in conflict, where the paradigm of Romans 7:14-25 is our daily experience: 'what I do is not the good I want to do; no, the evil I do not want to do – this I keep on doing' (Rom. 7:19).

Praying this petition of the Lord's Prayer, then, has in view the ultimate triumph of Christ in the gathering of the church, as well as the visible defeat of Satan in our own lives as we struggle with ongoing sin. Every victory against sin and Satan is an advancement for the kingdom of God.

But in a greater sense than this, the petition has in view not just the advancement of individuals, but the progress of the entire church of Christ. It is a missionary prayer! It is, in fact, a three-word formula describing what Jesus says in the Great Commission, following his death and resurrection. All authority is his, not Satan's. The church is therefore bidden to go and make disciples of all nations (the fulfilment of the Abrahamic promise!), 'baptizing them in the name of the Father and of the Son and of the Holy Spirit' (Matt. 28:19). That is to say, placing them under the authority of the triune

King! Disciples are subject to the reign of the King who is Father, Son and Holy Spirit. It is a kingdom commission, that must be in effect 'to the end of the age'. Jesus has asked the Father for the nations in accordance with the promise of Psalm 2:8 'Ask of me, and I will make the nations your inheritance, the ends of the earth your possession.' He now waits for all of his enemies to be made 'his footstool' (Ps. 110:1).

Capturing the cosmic extent of what God intends in this petition – what the Father will give to his Son, what the Father and the Son are accomplishing with the help of the out-poured Spirit – will transform our praying.

> Jesus shall reign where'er the sun
> Doth its successive journeys run;
> His kingdom stretch from shore to shore,
> Till moons shall wax and wane no more.[21]

5

GOD'S WILL ... AND OURS!

he third petition of the Lord's Prayer, 'Your will be done on earth as it is in heaven' (Matt. 6:10), brings into sharp focus that God is the chief concern of this prayer and not ourselves. Three petitions exalting God come first: *his* name, *his* kingdom, *his* will are to be our preoccupation whenever we come before him. This is in sharp contrast with much of our praying, revealing our prayers to be – too often – self-centred, egotistic, turned in on what we think are our needs rather than God's glory. The Lord's Prayer criticizes our praying, saying: 'Too often, you put your perception in the centre forgetting that God may have something entirely different in mind for you.' A failure to give God all the glory is at the heart of our sin-misshapen lives.

Trying to discern God's will can be difficult. Theologians, while insisting on the ultimate unity (or simplicity) of God's will, have talked about *two* wills in God. Some have distinguished between the *necessary* will (those things which God has to do because of his nature) and the *free* will of God (those things which he wills but does not have to from any determination of his nature).

Others have distinguished between the *secret* and *revealed* will of God, or the *decretive* and *preceptive* will of God. It reflects Deuteronomy 29:29: 'The secret things belong to the LORD our God, but the things revealed belong to us and to our children for ever, that we may follow all the words of this law' (Deut. 29:29).

Here the distinction reflects those things which God is determined to do (but about which he may not disclose to us) and the way in which that will (or a part of it) is disclosed to us who live in space and time. We need not be detained by these distinctions here, except to see that in this third petition, there is a recognition that a part of God's will is done on earth and another part in heaven. Ultimately, as the petition hints, God's will is one; there is no contradiction between what is true in heaven and what is revealed to us on earth, even though it may at times appear to us as though there may be. The third petition is primarily concerned with God's revealed will.

Though this petition covers the totality of God's will on earth, it will be helpful to focus on what that will may be as it concerns ourselves. In this case, God's will brings us face to face with the issue of *guidance*: how can I know the will of God and follow it?

There is an interesting study which we can do. Look at a Christian book written before the twentieth century and glance through its index to find what previous generations of preachers and teachers taught regarding *guidance*. The result of this study, you will find, is that our forefathers were not obsessed by the issue of guidance in the way many are today. Look at conference schedules and you will see that many are geared to the issue of guidance. Modern Christians are confused about God's will and its relation to their lives and are in constant need of help and reassurance. Why should we be so different from our forefathers in this regard? Is it because our lives are far more complicated than theirs? Is it because we have far greater variety of employment opportunities than they did? Or, is it because of the importance we give to leisure, thus raising moral issues of complexity that would never have occurred to past generations? All these have some truth to them, no doubt, but they fail to grasp the essential reason for the relative silence of past Christians on the issue of guidance.

So, what is the reason? What is *not* the reason is any notion that suggests that previous generations of believers were any less concerned with doing the will of God than our own. If anything, and here we speak generally, they disclosed a far greater desire to be conformed to God's ways than we do. The Puritans, for example, who seem never to have preached on the subject of guidance in any form that we would now recognize, were so concerned to discover the application of God's truth to the individual lives of God's people that they were derogatorily called 'precisionists' – a charge which one Puritan, Richard Rogers, responded to by saying, 'I serve a precise God!' No, the answer to this conundrum does not lie in the *desire* for guidance, but in knowing *how* it can be ascertained. Modern Christians are confused as to *how* guidance comes to us. It is at the level of how the will of God may be discerned that the difference emerges. Past generations seem to have had an answer to this that appears hidden to many of us.

How can the will of God be known?
'Guide me, O Thou great Jehovah, Pilgrim through this barren land...' Thus wrote William Williams in the middle of the eighteenth century and thereby expressed the longing of every sensitive Christian heart. But how can we know the will of God?

There are several answers that can be suggested. Some think that the will of God can be discerned through impressions made upon the mind or emotions, suggesting that one course of action is better than another. Usually, this leads to thoughts about God's will in terms of what best pleases us. Others think they have direct lines of communication with God and are therefore the subjects of impressions (on mind or spirit) that enable them to speak with confidence about knowing what the will of God is for their lives. Others read into unusual events the voice of God directing them in one way or another. Others try to obliterate the confusing noises all around them by making their minds 'blank' so that God may fill them. And many are just plain confused, unable to arrange the messages that come into anything that makes coherent sense: like 'white noise' or static in radio signals, the messages do not seem to contain anything that is clearly perceptible. The problem seems to be one of trying to point satellite dishes in the right direction in order to pick up the signals that God is sending. Some seem to have the picture clearly, or so they think; others do not.

But is guidance really this confusing? Does God intend for us to discern his will through a variety of impressions, urges, dreams and goadings of conscience? Is life really meant to be that subjective?

The answer here, as in everything else, has to do with how we view the Scriptures. Putting the Bible first will keep us from error in thinking and error in practice. Paul's view of Scripture, or rather, the Bible's view of itself, is this: 'All Scripture is God-breathed and is useful for teaching, rebuking, correcting and training in righteousness, so that the man of God may be thoroughly equipped for every good work' (2 Tim. 3:16-17). The goal of inspiration (or better, *ex*piration, since this is the meaning of the word translated 'God-breathed') is to instruct, convince, heal and equip us so that we might live the life God intends. It is Scripture that does this: Scripture read, Scripture preached, Scripture interpreted, Scripture applied, Scripture hidden within our hearts, Scripture lived out in our lives.

It is interesting that the Westminster Divines taught this when they came to write what was to be the first chapter of the Westminster Confession of Faith:

> 'The whole counsel of God, concerning all things
> necessary for His own glory, man's salvation, faith
> and life, is either expressly set down in Scripture,
> or by good and necessary consequence may be
> deduced from Scripture...' (1:6)

The totality of faith and life is to be deduced from 'the whole counsel of God...set down in Scripture.' There isn't an aspect of our lives that doesn't fall beneath the umbrella of what the Bible teaches. God's will is to be discerned from the Scriptures, either expressly or by inference.

'But wait a minute,' I hear you say, 'the Bible doesn't tell me which pair of shoes to put on in the morning, or who I am to marry, or whether I am to be a baker or a bricklayer, postman or physician!'

True, it doesn't. At least, not in so many words. But the Bible does give us principles by which we are to make these decisions. Our lives are to be ordered according to a set of rules that conform to the image of Jesus Christ. The Bible does tell us to use our common sense, and seek the advice and fellowship of others, and heed the voice of conscience. What regularly goes for some subjective nudge, this way or that, when it boils down to it, is no more than a conscience which has been trained to recognize God's way from the world's way. 'Whether you turn to the right or to the left, your ears will hear a voice behind you, saying, "This is the way; walk in it"' (Isa. 30:21). Yes, there are certain things – things we might call vocational issues – in which guidance does not come as a Bible verse saying, 'Walk this way...' Many issues in life will involve using our best judgment – judgments which have been honed by constant contact with Scripture and its principles.

Knowing where we are heading is the important thing here. Lewis Carroll's *Alice in Wonderland* puts it this way: Alice discovers a grinning Cheshire cat and asks: 'Which direction is it?' 'Where are you going?' replies the cat. 'I don't know,' Alice says. 'Then it doesn't matter!' says the cat. Knowing where we want to get to will determine what direction we will take. Without this compass, everything unravels.

Discovering God's will involves the following four things:

1. Asking what most glorifies God in any particular action and always choosing the best.

2. Studying Scripture to see what it has to say, either directly or by good and necessary consequence.

3. Using our minds and rational faculties: that is, employing the maxim of Psalm 32: 'I will instruct you and teach you in the way you should go; I will counsel you and watch over you. Do not be like the horse or the mule, which have no understanding but must be controlled by bit and bridle or they will not come to you'(vv. 8-9). Too many errors come at this very point.

4. Only having done these three things first should we then ask what 'burdens' God may have placed on our hearts, or what providence may have 'cornered' us into allowing no room but to go in a certain direction.

Several things need to be added to make this a more comprehensive plan of operation. We should, for example, always be patient when trying to ascertain the will of God. That God leads is a promise (e.g. Ps. 25:9, 'He guides the humble in what is right and teaches them his way'); but there is no promise that such guidance is always instantaneous. 'Wait on the LORD' is the Bible's constant refrain here (e.g. Ps. 27:14; 37:34; Prov. 20:22). Then again, we must always be prepared to discover that God's will may be the opposite of what we desire. Our emotions are not a safe guide and the wise Christian will not trust the voice that always speaks of ease and safety. That is why, by the way, it is never wrong, or an expression of unbelief, to add to our praying for the healing of the sick, 'If it be your will.' Praying, as Calvin insisted, is a covenantal work in which we pray for that which God has promised. When we have no promise, as in healing, for example, it is a sign of meekness, not *weakness*, to add, 'If it be your will.'

'Lord, what will you have *me* to do?'

It is one thing to know what the will of God might be, another to do it! What the third petition of the Lord's Prayer asks is that God's will might be *done*. The issue is one of submission *and* obedience on our part. There is a sense in which God's will is always done, and our part in this is to accept it. Praying 'Your will be done' in this case is asking God to give us humble hearts that we might not find ourselves complaining at the particular expression of his will that unfolds in our life. But there is a sense, too, in which the will of God calls upon us to *do* something, to be obedient to a particular directive. Praying 'Your will be done' in this case means asking for purpose of mind and resolve of spirit; strength, that is, to do as God bids us.

Both of these aspects emerge in the life of our Saviour in the Garden of Gethsemane. When he cried, 'Father, if you are willing, take this cup from me; yet not my will, but yours be done' (Luke 22:42), Jesus was revealing something intensely personal. Having withdrawn to pray, he had thrown himself prostrate on the ground and became so exhausted by the ordeal that an angel appeared to strengthen him (Luke 22:43). Resuming prayer (the Greek speaks of him being in 'agony,' *agonia*), sweat falls like drops of blood from his brow (Luke 22:44). The book of Hebrews, reflecting on this passage, speaks of the poignancy of Jesus' struggle: 'During the days of Jesus' life on earth, he offered up prayers and petitions with loud cries and tears to the one who could save him from death, and he was heard because of his reverent submission' (Heb. 5:7). It is a depiction of a man at the end of his tether as he reflects on the full implications of the will of God for the Servant of the Lord. We dare not minimize the reality of Jesus' request that, if it be possible, some other way be found for the redemption of God's people! Discovering afresh that there is not, Jesus resolves both to submit to and to be obedient to the demands now made upon him as God's will is made clear. Jesus' words, 'not my will, but yours be done,' are some of the most sublime in the entire corpus of Scripture.

Several important truths emerge as a consequence:

First, the instinctive recoil upon discovering how difficult the will of God may appear to be, is not necessarily sinful. There is nothing masochistic about Jesus' own handling of difficulty and trial. We are to take up a cross, he insists, thereby denying much modern thought offering health and wealth upon following him; never does he suggest that taking that cross will be anything but difficult and, on the surface at least, undesirable. Paul could pray three times for the removal of the thorn in the flesh, before learning that it was not God's will.

Second, acquiescing to God's will is hardly ever instantaneous; it is often a process of submission that takes some time. True, in our case, there is the intrusion of sinful responses: stubbornness, distrustfulness, anger and resentment, all of which make the process even more difficult. In Jesus' case, none of these are present, and yet there is a perceivable process whereby, through much conflict, he yields to the will of God. That is sublime! God does not disapprove of that part of the struggle whereby we are determining *for sure* his will. There is nothing stoical about Christian character in the face of trials.

Third, the will of God for our lives is hardly ever given in full at any one time. There is a sense in which Jesus knew the demands of his mission from the time of his childhood. Certainly from the time his public ministry begins, his assurance of the demands of service as God's Servant were clear: he unleashes three assaults on the devil's kingdom in the wilderness. Though it may appear as though the devil assaulted him, it is always Jesus who is in charge: the Spirit drives him into the wilderness in order that he might announce war against the kingdom of darkness (Matt. 4:1; Luke 4:1). But the full reality of his mission did not become apparent until Gethsemane. It is only here that the awful reality becomes crystal clear. God gives us sight of only so much of his will as we are able to take in at the time. It is the principle of the kingdom of God: 'Today's trouble is enough for today' (Matt. 6:34, NLT).

The issue, then, is whether we are willing to be submissive and obedient to that expression of the will of God that has become clear to us. In heaven, as the petition so wonderfully reminds us, God's will is perfectly done. There is no sin there to impede his will. But we are not in heaven – not yet! We are 'on earth' – code, that is, for that realm where opposition and frustration abounds. Hence the prayer that this world might more and more conform to that perfect pattern of heaven. It never will be true, not totally, that here on earth God's will is done perfectly. But in so far as it touches our lives, we long that it might be so.

It is a matter of putting God first.

6

DAILY BREAD

After I was first converted, my great consuming need, or so I thought, was a car. And I did what I thought the Bible expected of me. I prayed for a car. My prayers were simple and earnest: I didn't ask for a Cadillac, just a vehicle with four wheels and an ability to get from A to B without the need for an advanced knowledge of motor mechanics. Something dependable. And cheap! The Lord did not answer my prayers. At least, not at first. It was to be three years before I was in a position to purchase and run a car. I recall it well: it cost me, roughly, $50. It had done some 150,000 miles, I think, and it lasted all of three months. It died on a highway, unceremoniously belching out smoke that signalled its irrecoverable demise. I was on my way to preach and it failed to get me there.

I puzzle over that incident now, as I did then. Doesn't the Bible lead us to expect that God will give us what we ask of him? Does not the Bible say, 'Ask and you shall receive?' Have not Christian writers published books with titles such as, *How to Write Your Own Check with God.* Do not TV-evangelists insist that God's children are not meant to live in deprivation: this is God's earth for God's children. 'Name it – claim it' is their formula. So, why did God take so long to give me a car? And why did he take it away so quickly?

This story may not interest you to the degree it interests me, but I venture to suggest that it is a modern parable teaching some valuable truths. Of course, the answer, according to the modern counterparts of Job's comforters, is simple: my sin got in the way! And that is altogether possible. I do not wish to deny the very real possibility that the Lord did not hear me, because of my sin (cf. Ps. 66:18). But need it always be thus? Is the premise true, that God gives us whatever we ask of him, so long as it is 'in faith'? The answer to this is a resounding 'No!' It is to be found everywhere in Scripture, not least in this, the fourth petition of the Lord's Prayer. We are to ask for, and thereby receive, *daily* bread. But we are running ahead of ourselves. We first of all need to ask some more elementary questions about this prayer so that we may see what it *does* say rather than what it does *not* say.

There is a certain logic to the prayer: first, three petitions extolling God's name, God's kingdom and God's will underline the truth that life is meant to be lived for one purpose – to glorify God for all that he is worth. Now in the fourth petition, the tables are turned, so to speak, and we are concerned with ourselves. Having worshipped, we now ask for something. And the first thing we ask for is *strength to do the kind of God-focused living described in the first half of the prayer.*

Honour your bodies as the Spirit's temple

To some, the spiritual descendants of the third century ascetic and mystic Mani (his theology has been called Manichaeism), who believed that sin inherently adheres to the physical and that spirituality involves separating from the physical as much as possible, find a petition asking for food problematic. I am reminded of the witty words of Samuel Johnson who, when criticized for caring too much for his stomach, replied that those who did not would soon find that they were in no position to care about much else! No, the Bible is as concerned about the physical as it is about the spiritual. It is critical of those who care for the body and not the soul, but not in such a way as to suggest that the body doesn't matter very much. Indeed, the Bible witnesses to the fact that Adam reflected the image of God, not just in a soul-*ish* way, but in his bodily form, too (cf. Gen. 1:26-27). Jesus took human flesh – he was not an apparition or ghostly figure as Docetists such as Cerinthus taught, something which may explain the emphasis on Jesus' physical nature in John's writings. But, more especially, the Bible expects us to believe that the goal of God's redemptive work is the creation of 'a new heavens and a new earth.' Jesus may well have been alluding to this in his resurrection body whereby he ate a breakfast of bread and fish with the disciples (John 21:13; cf. Luke 24:30). What this brief sketch summar-izes is that God is deeply concerned about the physical body. He made it thus, and sends his Spirit to dwell in it as a temple (1 Cor. 6:19).

The fourth petition, then, reminds us that our salvation in Jesus Christ has a physical dimension. Our adoption as sons of God anticipates, Paul says, 'the redemption of our bodies' (Rom. 8:23). Though Paul argues elsewhere that what is raised in the resurrection body is 'spiritual,' it is, nevertheless, a spiritual *body* (1 Cor. 15:44). Paul is not denying the physicality of it; he is eager to emphasize that, on the one hand, it will be a body free from sin, and on the other hand, it is a body that is raised in power and glory. That is why Paul shows such concern for the body: he knows that in his body Christ is to be exalted (Phil. 1:20). Thus, Paul is concerned to mortify the deeds of the body (Rom. 8:13), even to the extent of keeping a watch over its parts, or 'instruments' (Rom. 6:13), so that he may present himself to God as holy *in his body*.

The fourth petition, in focusing on food, is saying: the body matters. We pray about the body and its needs. And more especially, God is concerned with our bodies. In the words of the author of Hebrews: '...we do not have a high priest who is unable to sympathize with our weaknesses, but we have one who has been tempted in every way, just as we are – yet was without sin' (Heb. 4:15). He knows how we are formed, he remembers that we are dust (Ps. 103:14).

This means that there is nothing *unspiritual* about praying for food, or clothes, or whatever else we may need in order to live our lives here in this world. We forget too easily that Paul was taken up for a good part of his ministry with collecting money for the believers in Jerusalem so that they could purchase food in the famine they suffered. And whilst the early church thought it unwise for the elders to be preoccupied with such things when other matters were more important (such as prayer and preaching), it showed its concern for physical needs when it elected men to serve as proto-deacons to administer food relief to the widows in Jerusalem (Acts 6:1-7). 'To wait on tables' may be less important on the scale of things than preaching the gospel; but it is not unimportant. The apostolic church ensured that it be done efficiently and comprehensively.

Then again, the petition has something else to teach us: in telling us that we should pray for bread – one of the most common food items, then as now – it is saying that we should pray to God *for everything*.

Trusting God for all things

What we have here is an argument from the lesser to the greater: if we are to pray for a loaf of bread, we must pray for absolutely everything.

Bread! Many of us have discovered the joys of bread-making! One of my friends naughtily calls it sacramental. What he means by that is that there is something about the whole process of making bread that reminds us of very basic things. Things like life and death. Yeast is alive and at certain temperatures, whenever it comes into contact with salt and sugar, the dough rises. Watching it can be fascinating. From very basic ingredients can emerge something which still sustains and nourishes in a way that, quite frankly, nothing else does. Bread still constitutes a basic food item in almost every part of the world.

Praying for bread is a way of reminding us that God is provider of all things; his providence is universal. To ensure that bread ends up on our tables, he must order the climatic, agricultural and economic conditions that ensure that bread can be produced.

Bread comes from the supermarket. True. However, there is a limitless number of factors that must come together to ensure that the supermarket can supply it and we have the means to purchase it. And the process whereby this is accomplished is covenantal. It is breathtaking to consider that God's covenant with Noah – that seed-time and harvest will not fail – lies behind a simple loaf of bread. Praying this petition for daily bread is praying that God will fulfil what he has covenanted (cf. Gen. 8:22).

Have you noticed how Jesus warns the rich about the difficulty of entering the kingdom of God (Matt. 19:23)? It is not impossible, of course. Abraham and Job were renowned for their wealth, to name but two godly folk in the Bible. And, were it not for the ministry of wealthy women, Jesus' own ministry would have been severely curtailed. The issue is not wealth in and of itself. The issue is one of godliness. Wealth makes it hard for a person to depend on God. If you are accustomed to getting everything you want, it is hard to develop good spiritual attitudes of a servant-like heart that waits on the Master to provide. Cyprian (c. 200-258 A.D.) wrote about the wealthy in his day in terms that shock us now as it must have then:

> Their property held them in chains... chains which shackled their courage and choked their faith and hampered... their judgment and throttled their souls... They think of themselves as owners, whereas it is they rather who are owned; enslaved as they are to their own property, they are not the masters of their money but its slaves.

That captures it well. Riches choke out the spirit of waiting upon God. They foster prayerlessness, ingratitude, and self-absorption. They encourage us to think of riches as 'my treasure' – to cite Gollum in J. R. R. Tolkien's epic saga, *Lord of the Rings*. There is a blessing that attends the need to have to pray for the next meal that outweighs the blessing of earthly resources. It helps us see that God is the giver of all good things.

Horatius Bonar caught it well in his hymn, *Fill Thou my life, O Lord my God*:

> Praise in the common things of life,
>   Its goings out and in;
> Praise in each duty and each deed,
>   However small and mean!

Even in the *mean* things, God is the great Provider. 'He loves thee too little, who loves anything as well as thee which he does not love for thy sake,' wrote Augustine. Seeing in a loaf of bread the sovereign providence of God is a lesson that is designed to keep us humble.

But why do we pray for *daily* bread?

Living one day at a time

It would be interesting if the prayer read, 'Give us this day our *weekly* or *monthly* bread'! Why did Jesus so word this prayer to ensure that we focus on the needs of one day at a time? Actually, the petition has been subjected to some severe analysis at this point. The original Greek uses a *hapax legomenon*, that is, the word translated 'daily' only occurs here in the New Testament. *The New Living Translation*, for example, suggests a marginal reading, 'Give us our food for tomorrow.'

Whatever the exact translation may be, the point remains the same: we are to pray for only sufficient bread for one day (whether it be today's or tomorrow's). The context helps us a little here. Bread is notorious for getting stale quickly. We moderns think we have cracked that problem through additives that prolong shelf life, but at the expense of taste and quality, some of us would argue. Hoarding bread before the days of deep freezers was a pointless exercise. But the issue is not really about bread, of course; it is about attitude. What this petition fosters is a spirit of dependence, of living a day at a time, of keeping short accounts with God. We are not to boast about tomorrow because we do not know what it might bring forth (Prov. 27:1).

In the setting of the Lord's Prayer in Matthew's Gospel, Jesus will proceed to teach about treasures and the futility of putting all our stock in this world, adding that we are not to worry about tomorrow, 'for tomorrow will worry about itself' (Matt. 6:34). It is interesting to think of this in terms of what Jesus taught in the third petition in which we are to pray for guidance, or better, for submission to God's revealed will. The problem with guidance is that we don't know the future! If God were to reveal more of it, we would find it easier to see what we are meant to do. Perhaps! But it would also, most likely, make it all the harder to submit to if that guidance contained hardship and suffering. It is a great blessing not to know what lies ahead.

Contentment

Contentment! This petition is a way of saying, 'Live by faith, one step at a time. Don't expect to know too much about next week, and still less about next year. Know that God will provide for what's ahead even though it may appear that the jar is running empty. Trust him.'

And that is hard. Hard, because we instinctively want to cushion the future. Protestantism has always encouraged saving and money manage-ment and forward planning. And nothing that is said here is meant in any way to discourage that. But the promise is for one day at a time and for those who forget it, God may bring them up short and remind them by causing their 'treasure' – not their true treasure, but their perceived one – to dissipate and shrivel.

The provision of *daily* bread fosters prayerfulness in a way that nothing else does. Sensing need around the corner bends us in servant-like shapes. Greed destroys. Wanting more than we need is what bends our lives out of shape. It destroys us; but it harms others too. We teach our children the difference between 'want' and 'need,' but we are slow to learn the lesson ourselves. We see others with their possessions and we envy them. Envy is followed quickly by resentment and bitterness. Death – spiritual death – is just around the corner. Hence the prayer in the Book of Proverbs:

> Two things I ask of you, O LORD;
> > do not refuse me before I die:
> Keep falsehood and lies far from me;
> > give me neither poverty nor riches,
> > but give me only my daily bread.
> Otherwise, I may have too much and disown you
> > and say, 'Who is the LORD?'
> Or I may become poor and steal,
> > and so dishonour the name of my God
> > > (Prov. 30:7-9).

There are few Christians who handle wealth well, just as there are few Christians who handle poverty well. That is why we need to be careful about embarking on a lifestyle that is designed to bring along with it increased temptations to conform to the spirit of the world. Be holy, that is, *different from the world*, is the Bible's exhortation to us.

'Give us this day our daily bread' is code language for, 'Lord, help me to be content with whatever you are pleased to give me. I will not ask for more than I need.'

7

FORGIVENESS

Bishop Ryle's book *Holiness*, which was first published in the last quarter of the nineteenth century, was reprinted in 1956 and has remained in print ever since. Surprisingly, it opens with a chapter on sin. The opening sentence has always struck me as an example of how to ensure that a book will never be read: 'He that wishes to attain to right views about Christian holiness, must begin by examining the vast and solemn subject of *sin*. He must dig down very low if he would build high. A mistake here is most mischievous. Wrong views about holiness are generally traceable to wrong views about human corruption. I make no apology for beginning this volume of papers about holiness by making some plain statements about *sin*.'[22]

He was, and remains, right, of course. Sin is the crucial issue in any consideration of the Christian life. Go wrong here, and everything else bends out of shape. Entertain light views of sin, and light views of holiness will be the result. To take sin less seriously than the Bible takes it is to fall into one of sin's most treasured qualities: *deceitfulness* (cf. Heb. 3:13). The church is too often taken up with all sorts of things other than a consideration of sin. The issue of today is self-worth, not self-condemnation. One popular TV preacher has caught the mood of the age by his oft-repeated slogan, 'Don't tell people they are sinners; it destroys their self-esteem.' Karl Menniger encapsulated the mood in a book he wrote in 1973 entitled *Whatever Became of Sin?*

There is something inherently negative about sin. 'Sin is a want of conformity unto, or transgression of, the law of God,' to cite the Shorter Catechism. There is the story of a little boy who was being quizzed by his father on the sermon that had just been preached. 'What did the preacher preach about?' the boy was asked. 'Sin!' came the reply. 'And what about it?' continued the father. 'He was against it!' the boy said. It is interesting that Paul puts it this way, too. 'The grace of God,' he tells us, 'teaches us to say "No" to ungodliness' (Titus 2:12). In fact, the Bible has many terms for sin, each one a picture word: sin is law-breaking, deviation, coming short, rebellion, pollution and missing the target.

David, for example, seemed to ransack the Hebrew dictionary to find ways of expressing what he had done in his adulterous affair with Bathsheba and the judicial murder of her husband Uriah that followed it. In the great psalm of repentance which is David's expression of grief at having disobeyed God by his behaviour, he puts it this way:

> Have mercy on me, O God,
>   according to your unfailing love;
>   according to your great compassion
> blot out my transgressions.
> Wash away all my iniquity
>   and cleanse me from my sin.
> For I know my transgressions,

> and my sin is always before me.
> Against you, you only, have I sinned
>   and done what is evil in your sight,
>   so that you are proved right when you speak
>   and justified when you judge.
> Surely I was sinful at birth,
>   sinful from the time my mother conceived me
>   (Ps. 51:1-5).

These five verses struggle to keep up with the richness of the Hebrew vocabulary, for they contain no less than nine key words, three about sin, three about the nature of God and three about forgiveness. The word 'sin' translates a Hebrew word which basically conveys the idea of failing to hit the target or of coming short. The word 'iniquity' goes deeper. It has the idea of fault of character lying behind the fault of conduct. It is a distorting, a bending out of shape. The third word, transgression, is stronger still, having the idea of a wilful rebellion, of knowing that a thing is wrong but doing it nevertheless. This is not a sin of ignorance, but what the Puritans would have called 'high-handed' sin. Three words reveal how God deals with sin: 'blot out...wash away...cleanse.' These words convey the deep-seated character of sin and express the idea that sin essentially separates us from God. Finally, there are three words about forgiveness: 'mercy, unfailing love and compassion.' The vocabulary of grace is equally rich. 'Mercy' signals the unmerited aspect of forgiveness, 'unfailing love' is perhaps the richest word in the entire Bible, enriched by covenant-theology that speaks of God's commitment to do as he promises, no matter what, and 'compassion' as a reminder that at the very heart of God lies a love that is not detached and cerebral, but passionate and flowing.

Debts

'Forgive us our sins,' the fifth petition asks (Luke 11:4), or, since the Lord's Prayer seems to have been given at least twice in Jesus' ministry, in the more familiar rendering of Matthew's account, the fifth petition is, 'Forgive us our *debts*' (Matt. 6:12).

Sin is an ongoing concern of the Christian life. Forgiven sinners are not done with sin forever – not yet! Sin is a *debt* we owe to God! Some wag once said that in a capitalist society such as ours, sin is best thought of in terms of a debt! We have failed to give to God what we owe: whole-hearted, unswerving obedience. Every failure to perform renders us culpable. In the words of Cranmer's Prayer Book: 'We have left undone those things which we ought to have done...'

The Bible motivates obedience by reminding us of our indebtedness: there is an *ought* that must be fulfilled, an *obligation* that must be met.

> 'This is how we know what love is: Jesus Christ laid down his life for us. And we ought to lay down our lives for our brothers' (1 John 3:16).

> 'Again I declare to every man who lets himself be circumcised that he is obligated to obey the whole law' (Gal. 5:3).

Some Christians balk at this. They suggest that because we are sons of God there is no obligation. In fact, according to them, obligation creates entirely the wrong impression of God. Indeed we are to relate to him as children do to their earthly fathers. It is a relationship of trust and love, they suggest. True, but this implies that obligation and love are mutually contradictory, which they are not. I love my wife, but does that mean I am not *obligated* to love her? I love my children, but does that mean that they are not *obligated* to me? Of course not!

Sin, then, is a failure to meet our obligations.

The first lesson that emerges from the fifth petition is that Jesus takes sin seriously. Anselm, the medieval theologian and scholar, wrote a treatise on the necessity for Christ to become incarnate in order for him to be our Redeemer – the book was called *Cur Deus Homo*, Why Did God become Man? In it, he portrays a somewhat dense character, suitably called Bozo, who cannot follow his reasoning. Exasperated, someone tells Bozo: *Nondum considerasti quantum ponderis sit peccatum*, 'You have not yet considered the greatness of the weight of sin.' A failure to take sin seriously leads us into all kinds of moral and spiritual failure. Sin, after all, is why Jesus came into this world. It is the reason why he had to become a servant – a *suffering* servant. It is sin that necessitated him dying on a cross of shame.

We can never take sin lightly.

> *Alas! And did my Saviour bleed*
> *And did my Sovereign die?*
> *Would he devote that sacred head*
> *For such a worm as I?*
>
> *Was it for crimes that I had done,*
> *He groaned upon the tree?*
> *Amazing pity! Grace unknown!*
> *And love beyond degree!*
>   Isaac Watts

Sinning again *and* again

A second lesson is this: sin is an *ongoing* issue for the Christian. What I mean by that is this: there is a sense in which sin is dealt with in our justification. The satisfaction that Jesus offered on the cross is sufficient to cleanse us and to render us acceptable to God. Count Zinzendorf expresses the thought this way in the well-known hymn, *Jesus Thy blood and righteousness*:

> *Bold shall I stand in that great day,*
> *For who ought to my charge shall lay?*
> *Fully absolved through Thee I am,*
> *From sin and fear, from guilt and shame.*

If that is true, if our sins are truly forgiven by reason of our justification, why do we still need to ask for forgiveness?

Surprising as it may sound, I am frequently asked this question. Why do I, as a believer, ask God to forgive my sin? Do I not realize that as a believer my sins are already forgiven? Justification is God's judicial act whereby he pardons our sins on account of what Jesus Christ, his Son, has done and accomplished on our behalf. Through justification we are made right with God. Through justification we are reckoned as possessing 'the righteousness of God' (2 Cor. 5:21; cf. Rom. 3:23-26). Christ, as the 'last Adam', rendered covenantal obedience to the demands of the law, where Adam, our father, failed (1 Cor. 15:45). Justification is the judgment of the Last Day brought forward into the here and now. In Zinzendorf's words: '*Bold shall I stand in that great day…*' There is no condemnation to fear for those who are in Christ (Rom. 8:1).

Why, then, do I still ask for forgiveness? Answer: because I continue to sin! This answer, though simple in itself, has not been obvious to all, even within the Reformed community. During the time of the Westminster Assembly (the 1640s), for example, a view was current that maintained that God takes no notice of the sins of the justified.[23] The motivation of those who held this view was laudable enough: to maintain what they saw as the certainty of the believer's standing in Christ. These Antinomians (those who did not believe Christians are obligated to keep God's law) lost sight of two things:

that there is a difference between the law as a covenant of works (which Adam failed to fulfil, but which Christ did) and the law as a rule of life (something Calvin, for one, saw clearly in maintaining what became known as the 'third use of the law'); and further, the distinction between justification (whereby God acts as judge) and adoption (whereby God acts towards us as a father). The point is that God expects us as adopted children to obey him and is displeased (and makes known his displeasure) when we do not. Any other view is plain silly and, more importantly, unbiblical. Thus the Westminster Confession safeguards the true view by saying:

> God doth continue to forgive the sins of those that are justified; and, although they can never fall from the state of justification, yet they may, by their sins, fall under God's fatherly displeasure, and not have the light of His countenance restored unto them, until they humble themselves, confess their sins, beg pardon, and renew their faith and repentance (11:5).

This is a far better way of understanding the place and significance of ongoing sin than other attempts, such as that of the Dutch theologian, William à Brakel, who suggested that in justification only past and present sins are forgiven (up to the point of our justification in time), future sins are not.[24] Justification, therefore, is an ongoing act, something which is continuously taking place. This plainly contradicts statements of the Bible which tell us that justification takes place *once* and once *only* (cf. Rom. 5:1; 8:30). The American theologian, W. G. T. Shedd, put it this way:

> The justification of a sinner is an all-comprehending act of God. All the sins of a believer, past, pres-

ent, and future, are pardoned when he is justified. The sum-total of his sin, all of which is before the Divine eye at the instant when God pronounces him a justified person, is blotted out or covered over by one act of God. Consequently, there is no repetition in the Divine mind of the act of justi-fication; as there is no repetition of the atoning death of Christ, upon which it rests.[25]

This is precisely what Jesus was teaching in the foot-washing incident that forms the prelude to the chapters containing teaching in the Upper Room prior to his arrest and trial. Amongst other things, John 13 describes in pictorial language the difference between justification and sanctification. 'A person who has had a bath,' Jesus suggested, 'needs only to wash his feet; his whole body is clean. And you are clean, though not every one of you' (John 13:10). Ongoing forgiveness is a bit like the way we might wash our hands and faces prior to going to bed, having had a bath a few hours earlier.

One implication of this petition is the need we have as Christians to keep short accounts with God. We are to pray today about *today's* sins. Letting sins pile up is a bit like what happens when, in our relationships with each other or in the family, we let the sun go down on our problems. Resent-ment grows, communication gets stifled, and bitterness and coldness follow in their wake. 'If we confess our sins, he is faithful and just and will forgive us our sins and purify us from all unright-eousness' is our great comfort here (1 John 1:9).

Conditions?

A third feature emerges from this petition by way of a qualif-ication: our sins are only forgiven so long as we forgive those who may sin against us.

An expansive comment is given in Matthew's Gospel on this in the verses that immediately follow the account of the Lord's Prayer: 'For if you forgive men when they sin against you, your heavenly Father will also forgive you. But if you do not forgive men their sins, your Father will not forgive your sins' (Matt. 6:14-15).

Some find these words difficult to accept. If forgiveness is conditional upon something we do, how can it be gracious? The answer is to distinguish justification from sanctification once again. It is the believer, not the unbeliever, to whom Jesus addresses these words. The bestowal of ongoing grace is determined by, and conditional upon, the evidence of a life of grace already present. Works in the Christian's life evidence grace in the heart of a believer. Without them, there is no evidence of rebirth, no testimony to the Spirit's presence. The parable of the Unmerciful Servant is designed to teach this very lesson (Matt. 18:21-35). To whom much is forgiven, much is required. The one forgiven much must be ready and willing to forgive others who ask him for forgiveness.

But is forgiveness on our part *unconditional?* Should we grant forgiveness, for example, to those who are unrepentant? This is no ivory tower scenario. Here's the situation: a woman has been brutally raped. The police catch the culprit and he is arraigned, brought to trial and convicted. There is no doubt as to his guilt. But at the sentence, he casts an evil eye at his victim. Some would-be counsellor now encourages the victim to forgive her attacker. 'You will not know true rest until you do,' she says. Whilst this may make psychological sense, is it the Christian thing to do? Many would insist that it is.

Now, we need to get one thing straight: if the attacker is truly sorry for his crime, begs her to forgive him, there is no ambivalence here: however difficult it may be, it is her moral duty to forgive. We forgive because Christ has forgiven us. But that is not the scenario we now envision. What then?

Hard as it sounds, some insist that the granting of forgiveness to the unrepentant is an unbiblical thing. It focuses on ourselves (our psyche in particular) rather than upon the true condition and ultimate well-being of those who have sinned against us. The most important thing for us to do in any situation is to seek the ultimate salvation of sinners. This can only be done by pointing out their sins, not by ignoring them. Salvation comes at the end of a process that involves conviction of our sinfulness and unworthiness. To hint that forgiveness may be possible without repentance is to fly in the face of the gospel way. *God does not forgive without repentance*! Jay Adams, for example, has written:

> It should go without saying that since our forgiveness is modelled after God's (Eph. 4:32), it must be conditional. Forgiveness by God rests on clear, unmistakable conditions. The apostle did not merely announce that God had forgiven men... Paul and the apostles turned away from those who refused to meet the conditions, just as John and Jesus did earlier when the scribes and the Pharisees would not repent.[26]

Others have taken the opposite position, insisting that forgiveness is never conditional. John F. MacArthur, for example, writes: 'To make conditionality the gist of Christlike forgiving seems to miss the whole point of what Scripture is saying.'[27]

Whatever view we take, one thing is unmistakably clear: there must never be on our part an *unwillingness* to forgive. Whatever obstacles there may be on the part of the offender in receiving forgiveness, we, on our part, must always be ready to forgive. Closure, to use a North American word, may not be possible. But the obstacle must not be due to some unwillingness on our part.

But there is another 'hard' thing here: that genuine repentance is more than just saying, 'I'm sorry.' We talk about apologizing, but the Bible doesn't use this word. Saying, 'I'm sorry' without admitting your sin is a cheap way of circumventing the Scripture's demands for honesty and integrity. Saying 'I'm sorry' and nothing else means that we are still holding the ball. What we need to say is: 'I have asked God to forgive me, and now I am asking you to do the same.' And in that case, the believer cannot refuse. He dare not refuse. True 'closure' will only come about as that forgiveness is granted.

Anything less is hypocrisy.

8

TEMPTATION

T his text is the last petition in the Lord's Prayer. This prayer, as we have seen, is a petition that contains much more truth than we commonly think it does; like a diamond it can reflect fresh light enhancing its beauty as we examine it more closely. It is a passage that teaches us not only about prayer but about Christian living. It is one of those passages in the New Testament that makes it so clear that praying and living are two sides of the same coin. Our Lord Jesus is giving fundamental teaching about prayer; but, he is also giving us fundamental teaching about those things for which we are chiefly to live.

The Lord's Prayer divides into two sections: the first teaches us things we need to know about God and the second teaches us those things which we are to know about ourselves. Knowing God and knowing ourselves is, then, the theme of this prayer. Putting these two things together sums up the entire corpus of things that we need to know in order to live for God. Indeed, so fundamental is this that John Calvin, in his twenties, began his famous *Institutes of the Christian Religion* in this very same way, by suggesting that 'Nearly all the wisdom we possess, that is to say, true and sound wisdom, consists of two parts: the knowledge of God and of ourselves.'[28] Knowing God and knowing ourselves is the sum total of what we need to know in this life to enable us to be godly.

What do we need to know about God? We need to know him as our heavenly Father, the Lord's Prayer says. Furthermore, we need to know what it means to hallow his name, to seek his kingdom and to seek his will in everything. Fixing our minds and hearts on these three principles summarizes for us those things we need to know about God.

In the light of these truths about God, there are three things we need to know about ourselves: our need for bread – which is an acknowledgement of utter dependence upon God for everything in this life; our need for ongoing forgiveness – because of (as yet) incomplete sanctification in this world (expressed as it is in the prayer in terms which urge our willingness to forgive those who trespass against us); and our need to be safeguarded against Satanic assault – something which is determined to end our relationship with, and commitment to, our heavenly Father.

Provision, pardon and protection are the three horizontal features of this prayer designed to ensure that we live the kind of lives God intends for his children. In a world that has its complications, a reminder that there are only three things I ultimately need in order to live for God's glory is what this prayer teaches us. It is the third feature, protection, in the form of deliverance from temptation and evil, that we are concerned with in this chapter.

The interesting thing about this petition is that grammatically it is in the form of a parallelism. That is to say, a statement is made and then repeated and developed. The first part of the petition says, 'Lead us not into temptation.' The second part develops it and adds, 'deliver us from evil.' There isn't just temptation; there is also the evil one to reckon with. Additionally, we have an example here of stating something both positively and negatively so as to emphasize the point. Seeing this leads us to consider the petition from both the negative and positive points of view.

Leading into temptation

'And lead us not into temptation.'

The word temptation is now almost universally used in a negative sense, meaning to solicit someone to do evil. That makes it difficult for us to understand such passages as James 1:13, which states categorically that God does not 'tempt anyone'. If that is so, why pray for God not to lead us into temptation? This assumes that God does lead us into temptation on certain occasions. The confusion arises because ever since the seventeenth century we have tended to use the word 'tempt' in this restrictive negative sense. But the word is capable of a positive rendition in the sense of 'testing'. And in Greek the same word is used of both senses. James, in the previous verse to the one just cited, uses it in this sense, the NIV and NASB translations choosing to use the word 'trial' instead of 'temptation' (as the older KJV did): 'Blessed is the man who perseveres under trial' (James 1:12). As J. I. Packer puts it:

> …temptations are Satan's work; but Satan is God's tool as well as his foe (*cf.* Job 1:11f.; 2:5f.), and it is ultimately God himself who leads his servants into temptation (Matt. 4:1; 6:13), permitting Satan to try to seduce them for beneficent purposes of his own. However, though temptations do not overtake men apart from God's will, the actual

> prompting to do wrong is not of God, nor does
> it express his command (James 1:12f). The desire
> which impels to sin is not God's but one's own,
> and it is fatal to yield to it (James 1:14f).[29]

Jesus by this petition intends more than a prayer against our faith being tested for its authenticity. He has in mind situations that might solicit pressure upon us to stumble and fall into sin. James alludes to this in a very similar way in the opening chapter of his epistle when he uses the word in both of these senses. 'Blessed is the man who perseveres under trial,' he says. Here, he is speaking of the way in which many things come into our lives that are trials or tests of our faith (it is the same word that is used in the next verse for temptation). Peter adds the word of caution that we should not be surprised by the painful trial that comes into our lives (1 Pet. 4:12). James recognizes that God delights to prove to us that our faith is real and genuine. The man who perseveres under the test, James is saying, is greatly blessed because when it is over he will receive the crown of life.

James adds, however: 'When tempted, no one should say, "God is tempting me." For God cannot be tempted by evil, nor does he tempt anyone' (James 1:13). Here James means by 'tempted' the particular solicitation that leads us to fail the test and to be drawn into sin. When that happens, God has no part in it. We are to pray that we be saved from that. It is in this vein that we understand those warnings of Jesus: 'Watch and pray so that you will not fall into temptation' (Matt. 26:41; cf. Mark 14:38).

Think of it this way: there are situations we may find ourselves in where the exit door is clearly seen and the way of escape evident. These are tests. Whenever God leads us into these kinds of situations, he always clearly labels the exit route: 'No temptation has seized you except what is common to man. And God is faithful; he will not let you be tempted beyond what you can bear. But when you are tempted, he will also provide a way out so that you can stand up under it' (1 Cor. 10:13). Temptation is not sin, for Christ was tempted as we are, yet remained sinless (Heb. 4:15). Temptation becomes sin only when and as the suggestion of evil is accepted and yielded to.[30]

However, there are situations where there appears to be no evident escape from the temptation. The allurement seems devoid of a way of escape. These are Satan's doings. The Bible yields a certain morphology to this kind of temptation. James, in the passage we have alluded to, is very clear here: 'When tempted, no one should say, "God is tempting me." For God cannot be tempted by evil, nor does he tempt anyone; but each one is tempted when, by his own evil desire, he is dragged away and enticed. Then, after desire has conceived, it gives birth to sin; and sin, when it is full-grown, gives birth to death' (James 1:13-15).

James is addressing two issues: responsibility and morphology. As to responsibility, the issue that we face is the same as that addressed in the opening chapters of the Bible where Adam and Eve end up blaming everyone but themselves for their sinful behaviour. James insists on unmasking the pretence, by insisting that we are responsible for our sins.

As for morphology, there is a deadly progression: from evil *desire*, to being *dragged* away, to *enticement*, to *conception*, to *birth*, and finally to *death*. This six-fold progression proceeds from the mind, to the affections, to the will, to the outward action and to a condition of spiritual death and enslavement.

One gets the impression that James was thinking of the story of David and Bathsheba in 2 Samuel 11 in his use of conception and birth imagery. There, too, in the sordid tale of David's adulterous affair with Bathsheba, Uriah's wife, there is an evident progression of sin that leads to death.

The story takes place at the time of year when men (like David) went forth to do battle (2 Sam. 11:1). His first mistake was to feel that he was above the responsibilities of an ordinary believer, being able to relinquish his responsibilities. He took advantage of his powerful office and thought himself above the demands that are made on individuals. Walking one evening on his flat-roofed house, he saw a beautiful woman, and instead of averting his eyes as he should have, he pursued the matter, allowing illicit desire to emerge. Bathsheba was a married woman but when he discovered this, it was already far too late for him to turn back: he had already gone too far because his lust had already got hold of him. Intercourse resulted in Bathsheba's pregnancy, the birth of a child and its swift death. David had crossed the Rubicon the night he allowed his eyes to linger; the point from which he could not return had been passed.

John Bunyan, in 1684, published a broadsheet, designed to be pinned to the wall of the house in much the same way we attach sundry things to our refrigerators. The subject matter was sin, and the piece was called *A Caution to Stir Up to Watch Against Sin*. The second verse of the sixteen-verse poem goes like this:

> Sin rather than 'twill out of action be,
> Will pray to stay, though but a while with thee;
> One night, one hour, one moment will it cry,
> Embrace me in thy bosom, else I die:
> Time to repent, [saith it], I will allow,
> And help, if to repent thou know'st not how.
> But if you give it entrance at the door
> It will come in, and may go out no more.[31]

And Jesus is teaching us to pray that we may be protected when we find ourselves faced with situations and enticements that would drag us away from loyalty to him.

The growing Christian grows in recognition of his frailties. It is one thing to have the desire to have those things which are contrary to God's will and never to find yourself in those contexts that would fulfil those desires. Often, it is only the lack of opportunity that keeps us from falling. When the desire and opportunity meet together, as they sometimes do, then we are sure to fall. And we need to pray that these two things be kept apart.

We need to recognize our weakness. We must never think that we cannot be tempted in certain ways. We must never say, 'That could never happen to me.' If we think like that, we have not made much progress on the road of sanctification.

> Do not flatter yourself that you can hold out against temptation's power. Secret lusts lie lurking in your own heart which will never give up until they are either destroyed or satisfied. 'Am I a dog, that I should do this thing?' asks Hazael (2 Kings 8:13). Yes, you will be such a dog, if you are like the king of Syria. Temptation and self-interest will dehumanize you. In theory we abhor lustful thoughts, but once temptation enters our heart, all contrary reasonings are overcome and silenced.[32]

Deliver us from evil

'But deliver us from the evil one.'

Jesus is now adding to this petition. We can be led into temptation and be made conscious of two enemies: the flesh and the cursed world. A corrupt heart and fallen world are enough to lead us to ruin. But it's worse than that. There is the cunning devil – Satan, to give him his proper name – who will employ the world and the flesh to bring you down.[33] You need to reckon with the devil. Twice in the New Testament, he is called 'the tempter' (Matt. 4:3; 1 Thess. 3:5).

Peter was told, 'Simon, Simon, Satan has asked to sift you as wheat. But I have prayed for you, Simon, that your faith may not fail' (Luke 22:31-32). These words are meant to be of encouragement and warning to us, too. Every Christian who is determined to live out-and-out for God can expect to meet the personal opposition of Satan.

But how will our heavenly Father deliver us from the evil one? Sometimes, he does it by acts of special sovereignty. He removes the circumstances or persons that have been the means of enticing us into sin.

Sometimes, he removes the desire. When we find ourselves in certain circumstances which are potentially soul destroying, he takes away our desire to yield to its allurements. The Holy Spirit makes us immune to sin's beckoning.

The Spirit's more normal way, however, is not to bring us such deliverances as these. He allows us to experience the full force of temptation's attraction because he wants to engage us in living the Christian life. He actually wants us to battle because it is through the experience of battle that we often grow. Just as unused muscles atrophy, so spiritual maturity is stunted by passivity. God wants to develop in us the skills of resisting the devil so that he will flee from us (cf. James 4:7; 1 Pet. 5:9).

But how, precisely, do we do this? And here we could expand at length. One thinks of the monumental work on this subject written by William Gurnall, *The Christian in Complete Armour*, in which he expounds on the passage in Ephesians where Paul speaks of battling against Satan, fully equipped with spiritual armour (Eph. 6:10-20). Another is the classic treatment *On Temptation* by the Puritan, John Owen.[34]

There is, however, a wonderful illustration of this in the Bible which is given to us to teach us this very lesson. We can learn from Jesus' temptations in the wilderness (Matt. 4:1-11). At the very onset of his public ministry, Jesus was delivered from the evil one.[35] By what means?

Several things are worthy of note in this incident that show us how Jesus had learned to respond biblically to every temptation.

1. He recognized the devil's subtlety. The devil came after forty days of fasting. 'Surely God wants you to eat. Why don't you just turn these stones into bread?' he opined. 'Use these miraculous powers for self-satisfaction,' he reasoned. Most temptations are subtle. In them, the evil one comes and says, 'It will be all right.' And it will not be very long before he comes and says, 'It's all wrong now, isn't it!' Satan is a deceiver!

G. K. Chesterton once suggested the following: 'If a rhinoceros were to enter this restaurant now, there is no denying he would have great power here. But I should be the first to rise and assure him that he had no authority whatever.' And the devil is like that! He pretends at authority, but he has none! We listen to him because he throws his weight about; but his voice is squeaky, and insignificant, if we but knew it. Jesus did!

2. Jesus reasoned with him. He charged him and rebuked him out of the Scriptures. It is interesting that Jesus must have loved the book of Deuteronomy. It is from this book (chapters 6 and 8, to be precise), that Jesus quotes.[36]

Jesus knew his Bible! He was able to respond and say, 'I will live in the way God has said.' Deuteronomy, sometimes called 'The book of covenant-renewal,' taught him to yield his entire life to God and his ways. Satan could have no part of it. *No part! And Jesus told Satan so.*

3. Jesus recommitted himself to his God-given destiny. Jesus had not come for himself: he had come for others, and especially for his Father in heaven. He had come, not to do his own will, but the will of his Father (Luke 22:42). Christians,

too, are to follow the same example: 'Not everyone who says to me, "Lord, Lord," will enter the kingdom of heaven, but only he who does *the will of my Father who is in heaven*' (Matt. 7:21). To say 'No!' to himself and 'Yes!' to his Father's will.

The grace of God, Paul reminds Titus, 'teaches us to say "No" to ungodliness and worldly passions, and to live self-controlled, upright and godly lives in this present age, while we wait for the blessed hope – the glorious appearing of our great God and Saviour, Jesus Christ, who gave himself for us to redeem us from all wickedness and to purify for himself a people that are his very own, eager to do what is good' (Titus 2:12-14). It is only as we say 'No!' in this way to Satan's enticements that we have in our hands the assurance that our heavenly Father is pleased to deliver us from the evil one. So long as it is an unresolved issue in my life, I am always going to be susceptible to that voice that says, 'Try this and you will enjoy it.'

After Jesus had resisted him, the devil left him (Matt. 4:11). He will leave us too if we follow this path.

Are you praying this way?

9

KINGDOM, POWER & GLORY

s with the concluding verses of Mark's Gospel, the concluding line of the Lord's Prayer, 'For yours is the kingdom, the power and the glory, for ever and ever. Amen,' is missing from most manuscripts that are available to us. Of course, no original manuscript of any part of the biblical canon has survived; what we have are copies, some citing a few verses only, dating from as early as the second century. This is a lot closer than any of the great secular books. For example, we can get as close as a thousand years to Caesar's *Gallic War*, to the writings of Herodotus and Thucydides over 1,300 years, and to the *History of Tacitus*, at least 700 years.

In the case of the New Testament, there are about 5,000 manuscripts available for study, in various languages and translations. The science of textual criticism endeavours to make judgments as to the exact nature of the canon. Estimates of variants in these manuscripts range into the hundreds of thousands, and the vast majority are easily recognizable as scribal errors in copying: missing out a letter, or even a line; repeating a word (dittography); confusing two letters which look similar; and the practice of inserting marginal comments which later became part of the received text. The science of textual criticism seeks to determine what the original text might have been. It is a perfectly laudable science and something that Christians who believe in the inerrancy of Scripture ought not in any way to fear. Nor should Christians be under the impression that they cannot trust their Bibles: less than 3% of the New Testament is in dispute, and no major doctrine is ever in question. Professor F. J. A. Hort, the nineteenth-century Greek scholar, put it this way: 'The amount of what can in any sense be called substantial variation…can hardly form more than a thousandth part of the whole text.'[37]

All this becomes relevant as we consider the 'Doxology' that closes the Lord's Prayer. The earliest commentaries known to us on this prayer, including that of Origen (c. 185–c.254) and Gregory of Nyssa (c. 335–395), inform us that most manuscripts available to them did not contain the doxology. Some manuscripts contained only a reference to the 'power and glory,' without the 'Amen' or the reference to the 'kingdom'. Whilst one of the Church Fathers, Chrysostom, argued for its inclusion, some of the most notable argued against its inclusion, including Tertullian, Cyprian and Augustine. In what is possibly the greatest Puritan commentary on the Lord's Prayer, written by Thomas Watson in the middle of the seventeenth century, no comment is given on the concluding doxology.[38] A similarly well-known commentary on the Lord's Prayer by Herman Witsius (1636-1708) does contain a brief section on the doxology which includes a bold attempt to justify its inclusion based on the (so-called) 'received text' as compiled by Erasmus in the early sixteenth century.[39]

Nevertheless, it has become so much a part of the Christian tradition, and its doctrine is so utterly biblical, that we are bound to make some comments on it. Some parallel statements in Scripture include the following:

> Yours, O LORD, is the greatness and the power and the glory and the majesty and the splendour, for everything in heaven and earth is yours. Yours, O LORD, is the kingdom; you are exalted as head over all (1 Chron. 29:11).

> The Lord will rescue me from every evil attack and will bring me safely to his heavenly kingdom. To him be glory for ever and ever. Amen (2 Tim. 4:18).

> Now to the King eternal, immortal, invisible, the only God, be honour and glory for ever and ever. Amen (1 Tim. 1:17).

> How great are his signs, how mighty his wonders! His kingdom is an eternal kingdom; his dominion endures from generation to generation (Dan. 4:3).

Nor is it difficult to see why this doxology might have been included. One such reason is liturgical. As the prayer became dislodged from its context, the doxology formed a fitting conclusion that makes the prayer complete in itself. Even in the context of Matthew 6, its inclusion marks off clearly the end of the prayer from the extended commentary that follows on the petition for forgiveness (vv. 14-15).

Doxology

All good theology should be doxological: it should seek to bring glory to God. For that is what doxology means: it is an expression giving honour to God. It is different from a benediction, in that a benediction expresses God's blessing to his people, whereas a doxology reverses that, giving blessing to God.

The Bible contains many doxologies. The most well-known are:

> to whom be glory for ever and ever. Amen (Gal. 1:5; cf. Rev. 1:6).

> to him be glory in the church and in Christ Jesus throughout all generations, for ever and ever! Amen (Eph. 3:21).

> But grow in the grace and knowledge of our Lord and Saviour Jesus Christ. To him be glory both now and for ever! Amen (2 Pet. 3:18).

> To him who sits on the throne and to the Lamb be praise and honour and glory and power, for ever and ever! (Rev. 5:13).

> Salvation belongs to our God, who sits on the throne, and to the Lamb (Rev. 7:10).

In the liturgical history of the church, the *Gloria in Excelsis* (based on Luke 2:14) was used up until the Reformation, when both Calvin and Cranmer omitted it in favour of the Ten Commandments. By far and away the most well-known doxology, still in use in the church's liturgy, is the *Gloria Patri* (based on Matthew 28:19f., and originating in the second century):

> *Glory be to the Father,*
> *And to the Son,*
> *And to the Holy Ghost;*
> *As it was in the beginning,*
> *Is now, and for ever shall be,*
> *World without end. Amen.*

Doxologies are essentially *praise*: praise to God for all that he is and does. As such, it forms an essential sub-set of all true prayer and worship. What Thomas Watson said about the relationship of faith to repentance, we can adapt for the relationship of prayer and praise: they are like the two wings of a bird by which we fly into heaven. Praise-less Christians are earth-bound Christians; only diseased hearts fail to praise.

We need to learn to fill our prayers with praises to the Lord!

> *Praise, my soul, the King of heaven,*
>   *To his feet your tribute bring;*
> *Ransomed, healed, restored, forgiven,*
>   *Who like me, his praise should sing?*
> *Praise him, praise him, praise him, praise him,*
> *Praise the everlasting King.*[40]

Resource and Reliability

The doxology is connected to the rest of the prayer by the conjunction, *for...*: '*For thine* (yours) *is the kingdom, the power, the glory, for ever and ever. Amen.*' Having asked for provision, pardon and protection in the preceding three petitions, the Lord's Prayer now asserts that the reason we may ask for such things is because our Father in heaven has both the resources and the reliability to give them. It is within both his ability and character to provide, pardon and protect because the kingdom, power and glory are his. We do not ask of one who cannot or will not answer us. Chrysostom puts it this way: 'After having roused us to the struggle by the consideration of the enemy, and entirely removed every apology for slothfulness, he again confirms and strengthens our mind by reminding us of the King, whom we faithfully serve, and by showing that he is more powerful than all.'[41]

The Lord's Prayer, thus, takes us full-cycle: having started with God, the prayer now ends with God. And he wants us to know that our praying is not in vain. He intends to answer us from the riches of his resources. God does not mock by inviting us to do something that he has no intention of heeding. C. H. Spurgeon once wrote:

> I cannot imagine any one of you tantalizing your child by exciting in him a desire that you did not intend to gratify. It were a very ungenerous thing to offer alms to the poor, and then when they hold out their hand for it, to mock their poverty with a denial. It were a cruel addition to the miseries of the sick if they were taken to the hospital and there left to die untended and uncared for. Where God leads you to pray, He means you to receive.[42]

Kingdom and Power

The first two words of the doxology, 'kingdom' and 'power,' are what grammarians call a *hendiadys*. That is, the two words are expressing a single, composite thought. We have already had occasion to mention the word 'kingdom' since it has been a part of the second petition: 'Your kingdom come.' It denotes God's all embracing control over all of his universe, but more particularly, his design to fulfil his redemptive purposes in redeeming a people for himself by overthrowing the rule and dominion of Satan. Having asked for God to bring that about, the prayer concludes by asserting its reality: the kingdom is *his*. As J. I. Packer puts it: 'Satan, the prime example of how sin breeds cunning but saps intelligence and rots the mind, does not accept that the Lord is king in this basic sense, and would dismiss this doxology – indeed, all doxologies – as false; but Christians know better, and praise God accordingly.'[43]

But what good is meaning without muscle, brain without brawn, intent without intensity? Rulers can be overthrown. Thus, we are reassured that the *power* is God's as well. He can do whatever he purposes to achieve. Job was brought low in order to confess it: 'I know that you can do all things; no plan of yours can be thwarted' (Job 42:2). As Jesus would say, 'All things are possible with God' (Mark 10:27). This last statement needs some interpretation to make sense of it. Theologians have drawn boundary lines: it is not that God can do *anything*: he cannot lie, or change his character, for example (Num. 23:19; 1 Sam. 15:29; 2 Tim. 2:13). We might put it this way: God can do anything that is within his moral and rational nature to do.

Knowing this is liberating and invigorating. It was this thought that drove the Psalmist to say:

> I love you, O LORD, my strength. The LORD is my rock, my fortress and my deliverer; my God is my rock, in whom I take refuge. He is my shield and the horn of my salvation, my stronghold (Ps. 18:1-2).

And again:

> God is our refuge and strength, an ever-present help in trouble (Ps. 46:1).

There is no power that can overthrow the rule of Almighty God. Jesus came into the world to destroy the devil's naïve claim to power (1 John 3:8).

What needs do you have? *The kingdom and power are the Lord's to provide!*

What sins have you confessed? *The kingdom and power are the Lord's to pardon!*

What temptations threaten to undo you? *The kingdom and power are the Lord's to protect you.*

Glory

'Glory' is one of those words we use as Christians without too much thought of its meaning and significance. Its Old Testament roots lie in a word which seems to speak of weight, or worth. When Moses asked that he might glimpse God's *glory*, he was given a sight of a burning bush that was not consumed in the process, together with an accompanying revelation of God's name – Yahweh (or Jehovah as we used to render it), a name which is later interpreted as, 'I AM (or will be) who I AM (or will be)' (Exod. 3:14-15; 6:2-3; 33:18–34:7). Later on, Moses asked to see God's glory again, but it was only God's 'back' that he was allowed to see (Exod. 33:23). The glory of God is beyond our ability to endure.

Glory was how the Israelites thought of God ever since Moses asked to glimpse his glory and God passed by as a bright, shining light – which later became known as the *Shekinah* – and ever-after was to be glimpsed (only by the High Priest) in the Tabernacle and Temple (Exod. 40:34; 1 Kings 8:10ff). *Glory* was understood as that which defined God's essential being. Thus, when John wants to tell us that Jesus is none other than the God of the Old Testament, he can find no better way as a Jew than to say, 'we have seen his *glory*' (John 1:14). Paul seems to be thinking of all of this when he writes to the Corinthians: 'For God, who said, "Let light shine out of darkness," made his light shine in our hearts to give us the light of the knowledge of *the glory of God* in the face of Christ' (2 Cor. 4:6). And John seems to be saying the same thing when he brings the New Testament to its close with the vision of Christ in the New Jerusalem: 'The city does not need the sun or the moon to shine on it, for *the glory of God* gives it light, and the Lamb is its lamp' (Rev. 21:23).

Glory then becomes synonymous with who and what God is. The doxology is therefore attributing, not only rule and might to God (*kingdom* and *power*), but also, in a sense, *divinity*. To say that all glory belongs to him is synonymous with saying, HE IS THE LORD!

But the Bible gives us a much fuller meaning of what giving or ascribing glory to God means. Take, for example, the following lines of thought.

We give glory to God by:

> 1. worshipping him: 'Whoever offers praise glorifies Me' (Ps. 50:23, NKJV).

> 2. trusting his promises (as Abraham did): 'Yet he did not waver through unbelief regarding the promise of God, but was strengthened in his faith and gave *glory to God*' (Rom. 4:20).

> 3. by confessing Jesus to be the LORD: '…and every tongue confess that Jesus Christ is Lord, to the *glory of God* the Father' (Phil. 2:11).

> 4. by our obedience to God's law: 'This is my prayer…that you may be…filled with the fruit of righteousness that comes through Jesus Christ – to the *glory and praise of God*' (Phil. 1:9-11).

Worship, faith, confession, obedience: demonstrating these in our lives ascribes glory to God.

For ever?

Ascribing qualities to God is what the Bible does from beginning to end. Its pages begin and end with God. Knowing his character is health-giving and enriching in the profoundest possible sense. But can we possibly understand that these are 'for ever and ever'?

No! This is beyond our grasp. We are time-bound and it is hard for us to imagine what a lifetime is, let alone endless existence. We find ourselves asking, 'How long is forever?' only to discover that the question is meaningless. 'But you remain the same, and your years will never end,' the Psalmist says (Ps. 102:27). But what does that mean? A great many modern theologians and philosophers read this as suggesting that God is 'within time'. But, our forefathers, men like Augustine and Calvin, were surely right in thinking that God is outside of time, that time is itself part of the created order of things.[44] God is not subject to the ravages of time; he has no yesterday or tomorrow. It is because of this that he is unchangeable, utterly dependable, always the same yesterday, today and tomorrow (cf. Heb. 13:8).

Our relationship with God as his children will never change, because God will never change.

Amen

Every Christian knows a little bit of Hebrew, for the word 'Amen' is a transliteration of the Hebrew word meaning 'firmness' or 'truth'. It's best known for the way Jesus employed it, repeating (in Hebrew style) the word by way of emphasizing some important truth he was about to speak ('Amen, Amen' or 'Verily, verily' as the King James Version rendered it). Jesus is called 'the Amen' in Revelation 3:14, since he is the faithful and true witness (John 1:14; 14:6).

Ever since Paul recorded that the early Christians added 'Amen' to prayers to suggest that what they say is true and dependable, Christians have done the same (1 Cor. 14:16). Saying 'Amen' to this prayer, the Lord's Prayer, is to assert one's conviction that everything in it is one's own conviction and longing. This prayer is *my* prayer. These petitions express the longings of *my* heart. This is my confession of faith, my record to what is essential and true.

I want to give reverence to the name of God.

I want God's kingdom to come.

I want God's will to be done above everything else and no matter what the cost.

I need bread, and I believe God will supply it because he is the Creator.

I need daily forgiveness, and the grace to forgive others, because God pardons through Jesus my Lord.

I need help against temptation and the Tempter.

And I pray in the confidence that all resources to give me these things are his, because he is the Sovereign Lord of glory.

I want God to have *all* the glory, just as the Shorter Catechism expresses it, 'Man's chief end is to glorify God.' All the glory!

I want to grow less and less that he might become all in all!

Is this your conviction?

Praying will take on a new life if it is.

REFERENCES

1. J. I. Packer, 'Some Lessons in Prayer,' in *Knowing Christianity* (Guildford, Surrey: Eagle Publications, 1995), 95.

2. Matthew Henry, *A Method for Prayer* (Fearn, Ross-shire: Christian Focus Publications (1712) rpt. 1994).

3. Isaac Watts, *A Guide to Prayer* (Brewster, Mass.: Paraclete Press, 1997).

4. J. I. Packer, *Knowing God* (London: Hodder and Stoughton, 1973), 182.

5. Sinclair Ferguson, *Children of the Living God* (Edinburgh: The Banner of Truth, 1989), xi.

6. John Calvin, *The Institutes of the Christian Religion* III.i.3.

7. Émile Doumergue, *Jean Calvin: Les hommes et les choses de son temps* (Lausanne, 1910), IV, 90-91.

8. Joachim Jeremias, *The Prayers of Jesus* (London: S.C.M. Press, 1967), 65.

9. *Institutes*, III.xx.36.

10. The *Sonship* programme was initiated by C. John (Jack) Miller for New Life Presbyterian Church in Jenkintown, Philadelphia in the early 1980s. It is an attempt to address the relationship of a Christian to the Law by highlighting the doctrine of adoption. For an analysis of the programme, see Chad B. Van Dixhoorn, *Westminster Theological Journal*, 61:2 (Fall 1999), 227-246.

11. *Institutes*, III.xx.40.

12. Herman Witsius, *The Lord's Prayer* (Escondido, CA: The den Dulk Foundation, 1994), 179.

13. I agree with Palmer Robertson that the use of *Yahweh* is problematic. He prefers the expression 'Covenant LORD.' See, Palmer Robertson, *Prophet of the Coming*

Day of the Lord: The Message of Joel (Darlington, Durham: Evangelical Press, 1995), 14-17.

14. *Institutes*, I.vii.4.

15. New Living Translation

16. Eugene Peterson, *The Message* (Colorado Springs, CO: NavPress, 1993), 20.

17. Colin Brown (ed.), *The New International Dictionary of New Testament Theology*, Vol. 1 (Grand Rapids: Zondervan Publishing House, 1975), 622.

18. J. D. Douglas (ed.), *The New Bible Dictionary* (Leicester: Inter-Varsity Press, 1962), 365.

19. John Murray, *Principles of Conduct* (London: Tyndale Press, 1971), 233.

20. John Calvin, *The Gospel According to St. John: Part Two 11-21 and The First Epistle of John*, translated by T. H. L. Parker, edited by David W. Torrance and Thomas F. Torrance (Grand Rapids, MI: Eerdmans, 1959), 124.

21. Isaac Watts' rendition of Psalm 72

22. J. C. Ryle, *Holiness* (Edinburgh: T & T Clark, 1956), 1.

23. Cf. J. I. Packer, *Among God's Giants* (Eastbourne: Kingsway, 1991), 204.

24. For a helpful analysis, see Anthony A. Hoekema, *Saved by Grace* (Grand Rapids: Eerdmans, 1989), 179.

25. William G. T. Shedd, *Dogmatic Theology* (1888; Grand Rapids: Zondervan, n.d.), 2:545.

26. Jay Adams, *From Forgiven to Forgiving* (Amityville, NY: Calvary, 1994), 34. Don Whitney, in a forthcoming work, *Ten Questions to Diagnose Your Spiritual Health*, takes the same position in a chapter entitled, 'Are You a Quicker Forgiver?'

27. John F. MacArthur, *The Freedom and Power of Forgiveness* (Wheaton, IL: Crossway, 1998), 118. In addition to these verses of the Lord's Prayer in Matthew 6:12 and the explanation that follows in vv. 14-15, he cites some additional passages, including James 2:13, Matthew 18:35, Luke 6:36-38. MacArthur seems to oscillate when he further writes, 'There are times when forgiveness should be unconditional and unilateral, and there are other times when forgiveness must be withheld until the offender repents' *Ibid.*, 119. Passages such as Matthew 18:15-17, he suggests, require confront-ation and repentance before forgiveness can be bestowed.

28. John Calvin, *The Institutes of the Christian Religion*, Ed. by John T. McNeill, Trans. by Ford Lewis Battles (Philadelphia: The Westminster Press, 1975), 1:35 [I.1.i].

29. *The Illustrated Bible Dictionary*, Vol. 3, (Wheaton, IL: IVP, 1980), s.v. 'Temptation,' by J. I. Packer.

30. *Ibid.*

31. John Bunyan, *The Works of John Bunyan* (Edinburgh: The Banner of Truth, [1854], 1991), 2:575.

32. John Owen, *Works* (Edinburgh: The Banner of Truth Trust, 1967), Vol 6, 105.

33. Older versions have 'evil' here, rather than 'the evil one', referring to the more generic concept rather than to a personal reference to Satan.

34. Op. cit. 88-153. 'Always remain alert to temptation's initial advice,' Owen exhorts, 'so that you may know when it is upon you. Most men do not perceive their enemy until they are wounded by him. Others, while noticing all around them those deeply involved in temptation, remain utterly insensible to their own danger. They stay

fast asleep, heedless of danger, until others come and tell them that their house is on fire.'

35. There is, of course, far more in this incident than a lesson to us as to how to meet the onslaughts of the evil one. Its primary significance is to record how Jesus took the initiative in meeting Satan at the very start of his ministry. 'The reason the Son of God appeared was to destroy the devil's work,' John tells us (1 John 3:8). Jesus emerges from the very beginning as *Christus Victor*.

36. C. H. Spurgeon once ventured the opinion, when, at the close of the nineteenth century, the book of Deuteronomy was particularly under attack by German critical scholars, that the devil was getting his own back from the havoc Jesus had caused him by this book in the wilderness temptations!

37. F. J. A. Hort and B. F. Westcott, *The New Testament in the Original Greek*, cited by John Blanchard in *How to Enjoy Your Bible* (Welwyn: Evangelical Press, 1984), 25.

38. Thomas Watson, *The Lord's Prayer* (Edinburgh: The Banner of Truth, 1960).

39. Herman Witsius, *Dissertations on the Lord's Prayer* (Escondido, CA: The den Dulk Foundation, 1994).

40. A hymn by Henry Lyte based on Psalm 103.

41. Homily xx on chapter 6 of Matthew.

42. C. H. Spurgeon, *Metropolitan Tabernacle Pulpit* (Pasadena, TX: Pilgrim Publications, 1981), Vol. 3, 251.

43. J. I. Packer, *I Want to be a Christian* (Wheaton, IL: Tyndale House Publishers, 1985), 176.

44. For an in-depth defence of this view, see Paul Helm, *Eternal God: A Study of God Without Time* (Oxford: Clarendon Press, 1988). The view that God is within time, or the 'Open-theism' view as it is now called,

is held by such writers as John Sanders, *The God who Risks* (Wheaton, IL: IVP, 1998), Gregory Boyd, *God of the Possible* (Grand Rapids, MI: Baker Books, 2000), and Clark Pinnock in *The Openness of God: A Biblical Challenge to the Traditional Understanding of God*, with contributions by Clark Pinnock, Richard Rice, John Sanders, William Hasker and David Basinger (Wheaton, IL: IVP, 2000). The view challenges the doctrine of God's immutability.

Other books of interest
from
Christian Focus Publications

Forgive Us Our Prayers

The Secret of Effective Prayer

JOHN HUFFMAN

Prayer is basic to our spiritual survival. To stay spiritually healthy we cannot afford to classify prayer as a low priority item.

Yet if God was listening to us pray, would we have to utter the words Forgive us our prayers...

Jesus gave us practical help to understand how to pray. From his own words we can learn how to change the way we pray for better. Through Dr. Huffman's study of 'the Lord's Prayer' we will discover fresh insights into the importance and centrality prayer should have in our lives – and if it isn't, how to make it so.

What is prayer? God has given us an amazingly powerful spiritual resource, modelled to us through the ministry of Christ. Prayer will equip us in our times of difficulty, help us praise at times of joy - it is the basis for our ongoing relationship with our heavenly Father.

John Huffman is Senior Pastor of St. Andrews Presbyterian Church, Newport Beach, California. He is chairman of the Board, Christianity Today.

ISBN 978-1-84550-051-1

When Grace Comes Alive:

Living Through the Lord's Prayer

TERRY JOHNSON

Terry reveals the spiritual depth of the Lord's prayer. Each subject is covered in depth – 'Actively praying for' – includes contrition, God's will to be accomplished, removing temptation etc. 'Attitude in prayer' – includes arguing our case before God, keeping an eternal perspective, the prayer covenant, pleasing God, reverence, etc.

This is a profoundly accessible book, one that cleverly combines the theology of the Lord's Prayer with down-to-earth application. Terry teaches us not only how we should pray but also how we should live.

Terry Johnson is Senior Pastor of the Independent Presbyterian Church in Savannah, Georgia.

ISBN 978-1-85792-882-2

Christian Focus Publications

publishes books for all ages

Our mission statement –

STAYING FAITHFUL

In dependence upon God we seek to help make His infallible Word, the Bible, relevant. Our aim is to ensure that the Lord Jesus Christ is presented as the only hope to obtain forgiveness of sin, live a useful life and look forward to heaven with Him.

REACHING OUT

Christ's last command requires us to reach out to our world with His gospel. We seek to help fulfil that by publishing books that point people towards Jesus and help them develop a Christ-like maturity. We aim to equip all levels of readers for life, work, ministry and mission.

Books in our adult range are published in three imprints. Christian Focus contains popular works including biographies, commentaries, basic doctrine and Christian living. Our children's books are also published in this im-print. Mentor focuses on books written at a level suitable for Bible College and seminary students, pastors, and other serious readers. The imprint includes commentaries, doctrinal studies, examination of current issues and church history. Christian Heritage contains classic writings from the past.

Christian Focus Publications Ltd
Geanies House, Fearn, Ross-shire,
IV20 1TW, Scotland, United Kingdom
info@christianfocus.com
www.christianfocus.com